I'm Called to Preach: Now What!

A User Guide to Effective Preaching

Dr. Aaron Chapman

authorHOUSE®

AuthorHouse™
1663 Liberty Drive
Bloomington, IN 47403
www.authorhouse.com
Phone: 1-800-839-8640

Published by AuthorHouse 11/26/2014

ISBN: 978-1-4969-5357-5 (sc)
ISBN: 978-1-4969-5358-2 (hc)
ISBN: 978-1-4969-5356-8 (e)

Library of Congress Control Number: 2014921289

Contents

After being turned down by an ordination counsel flat he
wrote his father a telegram one word rejected. His father
wrote back rejected on earth but accepted in heaven.

— Joel Gregory quote

Introduction

When was the last time you sat down on a Monday morning or evening to begin the process of creating an impactful sermon? Hopefully your answer was "recently" opposed to "quite some time ago!" If a humble and honest assessment was made, creating a sermon that permeated with purpose and power in its presentation more times than not would appear to be an insurmountable task at first glance.

Whether an experienced exegete or currently in the embryonic stages of preaching the Gospel, preparing to preach is not a painless process. As you prepare to start the Homiletic process, there may be a couple of preparatory thoughts that loom in your mind such as; "Sundays seem to arrive quicker and quicker; Here we go again; Didn't I just preach?; How do I keep up with this demand of preaching mighty, meaningful, messages?; What about this one?; Wow! quality sermons surely don't come easily." These thoughts I believe are frequent in the minds of those preachers who take seriously the mandate of sharing their convictions concerning the Word of God with a sense of passion and with exhausting preparation. It is my belief that preachers truly desire to prepare thought-provoking and inspiring messages weekly for waiting congregants but are at a total loss of how to do it effectively.

As you begin this journey, you will discover that some of the initial challenges presented to preachers are the following; (1) Where should I begin? (2) Where and how do I research the necessary materials? and (3) Which process will be practical enough and readily available to benefit them immediately?

Preachers stare at a blank sheet of paper, a blank computer screen, an IPad or Andriod Tablet weekly pondering what they should say or better yet where do they begin? This is where I found myself when I was called to preach at the tender age of eighteen facing my first sermon (this was fourteen years ago). This is the reason why I have decided to create this practical users guide for preachers to use as a walk through to help establish foundations, fundamentals and features of sound sermonic structure, while pointing them towards a more efficient methodology of sermon preparation.

If we were to make an honest observation of a preacher's homiletic vitals, we would find that most were ill prepared cognitively to develop theologically sound and spirit-filled sermons. This is evident when you have heard a preacher read a text publicly but never return to that text to effectively interpret the text. There are preachers that have misinformed other clergy by advising them (knowingly or unknowingly) to just stand up and tell the story, or how about the old adage open up your mouth and the Lord will give you what to say. I feel no dissonance informing you that it's not going to happen!

You need the guidance of the Holy Spirit along with a methodology or a paradigm to assist you in articulating the theme and thesis of a passage in a clarion fashion while conveying thus says the Lord!

I have been privileged to read several books which were rich in content which I attributed to the shaping of my homiletic lens: "*The Sound of the Trumpet*" by Samuel Proctor, "*How Shall They Preach*" by Gardner Taylor, "*Preaching*" by Fred B. Craddock, "*Preaching without Notes*" by Charles Koller, "*Living Water for the Thirsty Soul*" by Marvin McMickle, and many other practical and scholarly text that have impacted my framework of preaching. It is very admirable that these poignant preachers and homiletic geniuses felt it not robbery to share with other clergy their convictions for preaching and proven technique for textual interpretation. The preacher in them makes the preacher in me leap as John the Baptist leaped in Elizabeth when encountering Jesus. These pillars, Proctor, Taylor, McMickle and alike have inspired me to offer this feeble text to my own generation of preachers and those who follow.

Another reason I felt compelled to write this text was because I have not yet discovered a contemporary text on preaching that concerns a more argumentative style of preaching that I have become accustomed to and have a great affinity for at this present time. This type of preaching used the methodology of questioning the text aggressively and interrogatively to assist in your exegesis to unearth revelations from God in the scriptures. Let me be clear from the outset. I am not speaking of off the wall theological rhetoric and hunches with a border-line of heresy and definitely not eisegesis. I am an advocate for exegesis that is meaningful and relevant that can hold its weight in theological integrity and accuracy.

I know this book is not for everyone because some preachers are not interested in different techniques because of their ruminant routine while some do not possess a never ending hunger to find new ways to communicate the profound story of reconciliation through the rupturing of a savior on a rugged cross so as to reach sinners where they are. Preachers must understand that all because we crack the golden seals of the pages of scripture, it is not a promissory note for a sermon to land safely on the runway of salvific results. The day has come when preachers must get back to the basics of a true hunger for the word and preaching without compromise. In this text it is a basic guide on "How to" prepare an effective sermon from Monday through Friday. We will use as our nucleus or core question for this fundamental theological framework "I'm called to preach-- now what"? This question is reverberating and burning within the minds of preachers after receiving and accepting the call to preach. Wondering what are the steps to accurate sermonic delivery?

Preaching with Passion

There are several significant techniques, ideas, and types of wisdom that a preacher can share with other aspiring preachers. One vital component that a preacher cannot gift to another preacher is the passion for preaching. This passion or inward appetite to preach is not inherit but rather self driven. Passion has been articulated by Quincy Jones as an uncontrollable enthusiasm. It is the pure love and infatuation with your assignment given from God and the infatuation with the God that has given the gift! You must have both of these elements they are inseparable.

When you are passionate about preaching you desire to do it in season and out of season as Paul informed Timothy in 2 Timothy 4:2 NRSV. When you have a pure permeating passion for preaching there is a craving to be around it. There should be a spirit with-in that seeks out opportunity to hear preaching. As a preacher you should see it as advantageous to take the time to research it and those who have mastered the intrinsic structure of it. Those who are passionate about preaching will examine the techniques and methodologies of how to be more effective in articulating the gospel. Let me ask you are you willing to attend seminars and read books on the topic of preaching. Those clergy who have a true desire to invest in their preaching ministry can't stop thinking about it, they dream about it, they proverbially eat and sleep preaching as they strive to maintain precision in your calling. Preachers who are passionate refuse to take shortcuts to shortchange the process.

Preaching with a Lethargic Mindset

Mack Carter once said quoting one of the English preachers comically but yet seriously that "Sermons are extracted effectively when it comes from heaven and makes a detour through the buttocks to your head and that is because when you sit your buttocks in a chair and study then an inspiring sermon will come to your head."* Thomas Edison stated that "Genius is one percent inspiration and ninety nine percent perspiration." In the gospel ministry, we have adopted this phrase and come to the consensus that preaching is ninety percent preparation and ten percent inspiration.* These mindsets toward the perfecting of ones craft are contrary to preachers whose cognition is fastened only on having charisma but having no confidence in the process of preparation for powerful pulpit presentation. Martin Luther King in his book "*Strength to Love*" stated that it pains (men and women) to think. (King 1963, 14)

Unfortunately, the climate of ecclesiastical nomenclature for clergy has become a pirating of preaching poignancy. Preachers are confiscating sermons from the internet, convention expo tables of the up and coming preachers; preachers have stolen manuscripts from pulpit podiums following the preachers sermon (without consent) and they've hired ghost writers. Sermons have been preached directly from books and some preachers have even gone as far as bringing the book wherein they'd stolen the sermon from into the pulpit with them where it is on full display!

Theological thievery has become all too known and accepted. These misguided and mischievous preachers are lingering in their laziness refusing to study because they do not value hearing God speaking directly to them in that precious private time devoted to God as he provides us with pearls to drop on the pages. When preachers capture this disposition, they do what Gardner Calvin Taylor calls robbing the world of the true Gospel according to your personality!

You can never create sermons of value if you don't value the process of sermon preparation or if you never hunger to know a methodology of crafting sermons that are permeating with providential breath through your presentation.

Push toward the limits of your Potential

One of my favorite devotional writers Myles Monroe in his book *Maximizing Your Potential* spoke about the danger of being in competition with others concerning the potential you have because we might possess more capacity than we realize.

Clergy can't afford to lose the battle of sermon preparation in this postmodern generation. In order to succeed in effective communication of the gospel we need to prioritize our pre-sermonic prep. We need to embrace a *tabula rasa* a clean slate of the mind. Samuel Proctor suggests, after we've engaged in shedding the worries, the advertisement, the social media and our own preconceptions of ourselves then we are ready to push toward the endless limits of our potential in sermon preparation. Sermonic stretching removes us from just sermonizing and we find shades of stability and anchorage in spiritual formation. The preacher must examine his/her own personal life and examine their mortifications and motives for the preachment of the word of God. This medatatio scriptura, as Richard Foster calls it in meditation, only comes through focus and deliberate daily devotionals. (Foster 1988,*10*)

It was cited of Ralph Waldo Emerson commemorating his historic address to the Divinity School in 1838 where he said "Acquaint thyself with the Deity, As much as men are able to appropriate the Divine Mind." (Taylor 1977, 24) As I articulated in my book entitled *Preaching Without Heart,* quoting A.P. Gibbs "We cannot divorce the preacher from his/her preaching. In every real way the man (woman) is his message: the preacher is his/ her proclamation and the speaker is his (her) sermon. (Gibbs 2002, 31)

There is a necessity to understand the psychological strength of the preacher before preparation. There is a small voice ruminating that will attempt to tell you let's take a break today; you can do this at another time; let's just put it off Sunday is days away. Noel Jones in his DVD *Preaching 101* which was filmed at the Potters House in Texas stated: "You have to study it is like working out, if you miss it you will feel guilty!"

The greatest enemy to preparing impactful sermons is procrastination. For you to remain disciplined daily you must combat the evaporation of your work ethic because of an unyielding determination to improve daily. Of course everyone desires to lay down and rest (and at the appointed time you should rest to remain vibrate and healthy) but, there must be a consciousness in the mind of the preacher that issues will always arise

To misguide the advancement of your preaching craft and ministry. Growth will be left forever groaning for the fuel of commitment when you perpetually wake up late, watch television frequently, electronic apps miscarry your motivation while you're engaged in playing angry birds for hours, words with friends, and hanging out with pastor or preaching pales and engage in comical preacher conversation over breakfast; but have you ever considered what will this habitual scheduling of your time produce.

Believe me there is nothing heretical about having down time to relax and regain focus for the task of engaging in what Richard Foster calls the prayer of rest (remaining still and silent before God) but, when this becomes a frequent occurrence it will chip away at the edge you have developed mentally to maintain rigorous sermon preparation. Truthfully the lack of using potential filled days will perpetually produce ill prepared Saturday night or Sunday morning specials which results in the minister engaging in malpractice in the pulpit and meaningless meandering producing messages of mediocrity.

I believe God has imbued in every preacher talents and gifts that others do not possess. In this book I do not claim that these tools can empower any preacher if you don't have the learning, burning, and the calling. However, if you possess these three I can provide principles of preaching to practice for a better pulpit presentation and road map to progress. Now, turn the page and lets proceed with the first step in how to gain precision in our preaching!

Inspiration is easy. Implementation is the hard part.

Bob Taylor

Don't Despise the Process

Chapter 1

To every initiation of adventure or new trend toward a valuable task there is a learning curve which most people will encounter. To overcome this curve and become effective in ones craft there must be a steady work ethic to enhance the preachers development. Richard Foster suggested concerning the discipline of study that "Discipline in study is the primary vehicle to bring us to think about quality things."(Foster 1988 62) Regardless if a person is among the category of the elite, or if they are extra gifted, charismatic, and talented we must all start from a coordinates of conception known as curiosity. I believe we should remain mindful from the out-set that there are no fulfilling short cuts to quality sermonic preparation. If you can, grasp the fundamental mindset that Michael Jordan spoke passionately about in one of his Nike commercials which was *you won't receive anything if there is no "work before glory."* This whole notion of work before glory is profitable for us to ponder--not because we are searching for vain glory for what we do in pulpit ministry but because we realize that all glory belongs to God;

As Clergy we should have discovered that we cannot inculcate the grasping of fulfill-ment in ministry while ministering to God's people in power and ignore the profundity of pedagogical practice.

If there is no intentionality in investigating the under girding theme of these sacred text we will be found wanting for sermons that are solid and effective. John Maxwell challenges us in our dispositions of holding on desperately to our former melliferous moments in ministry by stating if what you have done yesterday still looks big today then you have not done enough today!

As an experienced preacher, there is a habit to preach on the residue of sermonic delivery that has been successful in the past. While this practice sometimes is needed to help the preacher gain ground through the oasis of rest; it can also paralyze your pattern of rigorous preparation which could lead to staunched mental and spiritual growth due to the absence of the all important weekly spiritual stretching which occurs during preparation. The greatest temptation to the preacher is to recline, to shine, and whine (Taylor 1977, 33).

The preacher must fall in love with the one in whom he is preparing with (God) then fall in love with those in whom he is preparing for (the people) and finally fall in love with the preparatory moment itself. There was a joke told by Charles Spurgeon wherein he stated the English preachers have said that they have studies while the American preachers have offices because there is no studying being done in American preachers offices. Another allegation against American preachers is the insatiable desire to spend great amount of money on their car's but won't spend a dime on their libraries. We must take the time in pain staking critical study to attempt to master our gifts of proclaiming God's word. Gibbs stated study is the price that must be paid for knowledge; every preacher must be prepared to pay the price or he/she will never become a worthwhile preacher or teacher of the Gospel, (Gibbs 2002, 43). Fred Craddock compliments what Gibbs speaks about by advising preachers that "Study will protect the parishioners from the excessive influence of the minister's own opinions, prejudices, and feelings. Study is getting a second and third opinion before diagnosis and treatment"(Craddock 2010, 70).

Every preacher must build a resistance to the pains of preparation in order to stretch themselves further. While seated in preparation you have to push beyond the grueling thoughts of the hours you have put in and say to yourself just one more hour; after researching and it seems as though you have went to the bottom of the barrel of information you have to push yourself to grab one more book off the shelf or download one more resource. When you have become literally exhausted from preparation, can you fight and get one last prayer or thought? In this comes the breaking point and after conquering it comes the blessing point and this is where you find God is waiting on the other side for you! Many quit on the edge of his glory instead of pressing their way through preparation and basking in the euphoria of this intimate moment shared with God. John Maxwell equated this mindset to the second wind of a track runner he stated:

> **A track star who runs a long distance learns to depend upon his "second wind." He runs until he's weary and exhausted. But he doesn't stop there. The average runner decides to quit, but the track star knows that if he can endure a little more pain, he'll get this "second wind." Until a person tried hard enough and long enough to get his second wind," he'll**

never know how much he can accomplish. Remember: ability is 95 percent "stickability". (Maxwell 1999, 48)

Overcoming deficiencies

Being a great preacher is not based upon the extremity of giftedness but a desire that is unquenchable to do an uniquely unequivocal work for God. According to James Massey while quoting Walter Russell in his book *Designing the Sermon,* "The real preacher, is more than a maker of sermons He is a medium of contact between God and the minds and hearts of men." (Massey 1980, 15)

There are some preachers that are defeated prior to them even stepping into the pulpit because they don't possess the faith and the confidence that they can be a catalyst or conduit for Christ to communicate his gospel effectively. What some preachers call writers block in all actuality is confidence block.

We must be convinced in our private moments of preparation that God will gift us with illuminating insights for their injured circumstances so his people can be the benefactors of our rigorous moments of theological reflection. Let me raise for your consideration: Do you begin your preparation by saying "I can't do this, what is the use? I will never get this; I am wasting my time." If you are saying this and recapitulating it in your mind you are correct according to Proverbs 23:7 NRSV "For as he/she thinks in his/her heart, so is he/she". Gibbs stated "Someone has said study consists of the application of the seat of the trousers to the seat of the chair, until such time as the subject has been mastered." (Gibbs 2002, 41)

In a motivational speech given by Will Smith he stated that "the separation of talent and skill is one of the greatest misunderstood concepts for people who are trying to excel. Talent you have naturally (skills) is only developed by hours and hours of beating on your craft."(Smith 2011 Talent Skill Success You Tube Video)

This misnomer that the reason why a preacher is excelling is based on gift and talent is simply a lie. It is those preachers who refuse to allow any of their capacity and potential to be wasted. Therefore it is these individuals that have the mental capacity to push themselves beyond the limitations set by others expectations and mindsets because as one writer suggested there are times God is waiting to use someone in history that is ignorant of the impossibilities and use them to make the impossible possible. You must understand that God has called you in order to use you in a mighty way.

It is a common knowledge that every person is not the same. There are some people that have physiological challenges, psychological challenges, or even emotional Challenges. There are those who have ADHD but they concentrate and study even more to make sure they can convey the gospel effectively. Some preachers have speech impediments and they go through exercises to get help to articulate to their maximum ability. They've shook the world with their sermonic delivery and saved many souls for the Savior. This is to say don't despise any challenge that may be attempting to kidnap your level of confidence to prepare and proclaim God's word with purpose.

You must be driven and devoted to the process of preparation. If there are those who've overcome their obstacles then what is our excuse? Here are some further examples:

There are several inspirational moments from challenged individuals that are etched in the hearts of those who will never give up because of difficulty. The first was that Brazil protégé who was handless who grew up watching his father carving sculptures out of wood and who watched his technique carefully. He side stepped the excuses of not having the physiological faculties and equipment to do what he loved because he lost his hands to leprosy. He was so determined to learn the trade that he learned to carve with his feet and he has become the inspiration of Brazil carving several sculptures but known most for his sculpting of 12 life size Old Testament prophets. This protégé does this with no hands and most of us have two good hands and two good feet and choose not do anything with our purpose.

Erin Hayes gives us another reality story of inspiration concerning a young man who is now 18 years of age, blind from birth, has shrunken limbs and he's wheelchair bound. He learned to play the piano and makes the trumpet sing eloquently with melodious tunes without sight and with nubs for limbs; he stated profoundly about his condition "God made me blind big deal" it is nothing to remain down and depressed about.

How about that prodigy of the civil rights movement Martin Luther King Jr. who was affected by that tragic incident which happened while he was at a book signing for his first published book *"Stride Toward Freedom"*. A frantic, fickle female who was frustrated with the furthering of the civil rights movement stabbed Dr. King with a knife and the tip of the blade was lodge just on the edge of his aorta and if it had punctured it would have resulted in him internally drowning in his own blood! After the diagnosis and prognosis he discovered if he would have sneezed he would have severed that aorta and died. A high school girl from White Plains high school wrote him a letter stating these words "I'm so glad you didn't sneeze". He was inspired to give rise to this incident in his last speech prior to being murdered in Memphis. All of these individuals had their own separate challenges but they didn't despise the process which allowed them to come into their destiny and you can do the same.

We cannot circumvent pain for us to receive the progress that we search for in Preaching. Arnold (Schwarzenegger) spoke about a comment that the former heavy weight boxing World Champion Muhammad Ali stated during his training was that he doesn't count reps until he feels pain! Muhammad Ali stated that nothing really counts until after pain. You have to take the pain of preparation to move from who you are into who you can be in your life! Pain is just a part of the process. Eric Thomas, a renowned motivational speaker once said why give up now, you are already in pain then why not get a reward from it! If we want to become effective we can get to our destination but we cannot skip paying the tolls (the price) to get there.

Living a life of Wellness

There are too many preachers that abuse their body through a lack of rest, do not exercise and who fail to eat food appropriate for fueling their flesh which short circuits their best chance of preaching

7

at their maximum potential. I am an advocate for exercising the body in conjunction with exercising the mind. Whenever you play sports or if your schedule calls for you to travel several places week in and week out this can begin the imperceptible dwindling of your health. You have to come to the understanding as Paul stated that your body is the temple of God. How do we honor God with what we allow to come into the body He has made. Also how are we doing on our stewardship of that body to make sure that it is performing at its peak? We must Exercise! I advise anyone to see your physician regularly for check ups and see what exercise program would fit you best.

There are various exercises that can help with endurance during your preaching such as the treadmill which helps your wind and allows oxygen to flow freely in the body. Another exercise is sit ups, this helps the abs so you can pull wind effectively from your stomach. Lifting weights keeps the heart rate going and strengthens the body. Exercise plays a great role in the longevity of your preaching ministry. If you neglect the importance of it you can find yourself on your back or in your grave from a stroke or heart attack therefore, take care of the body the Lord has given you!

Obtaining a Mental Discipline

One of the most underestimated elements to preaching is the importance of mental stability. To those who have not been in ministry long or have just embarked on the journey, there is a mental pressure that you have to endure to keep up with such a regiment. Across the country there are pastors that preach at least three times a

Sunday not including the invitations to other churches. This schedule comes with unceasing expectations that the preacher should have a larger than life anointed output for every message when he or she mounts the pulpit.

The preacher who is under constant demands to deliver effectively with timelessness must have a way of remaining fresh so that his or her preaching doesn't become bland or dry. The best methodology that one can use is to frequently acquaint ones self with the search of scripture. Stephen Rummage offers an important insight when he suggested. The preacher who has steeped himself in the bible will have a clearness of outlook which will illuminate many dark things, and firmness of touch which will barred confidence in him among his hearers. He will have the secret of perpetual freshness, for he cannot exhaust the Bible. (Rummage 2002,19)

To remain crisp as clergy we need to engage scripture but we also need to clutch to our personal relationship with God. While attending a ministerial seminar the topic was given rise concerning the right way to approach burnout in ministry. E.L. Branch gave the response that when dealing with ministry burn out the best way to handle that burn out is to not pull away from God but to cling closer to God through praying and the reading of God's word. It is in the personal relationship that our preaching finds its strength and stability to minister to an instable world. When we view preaching many words we use to discuss preaching are nouns (e.g., proclamation, sermon, homily, homiletics, the word, interpretation) rather than verbs stressing action and personal relationship. The personal relationship in our preaching should sooth clergy to continue ministering to the people of God even if their struggles are flagrantly personal they can survive the season of lows and still yet deliver messages with power. That is mental strength!

The Last thing I want to share is the challenge mentally of forever chasing ourselves. In our minds eye we don't need to become guilty of chasing others that we are already light years ahead of. There are times in our ministry that we find ourselves dwelling to often on our recent success which makes us comfortable. This becomes tragic because there are times that the successful preacher that we've been in the past actually begins to suffocate the preacher that is trying to be birthed in the future. We have to understand the importance of forever evolving in ministry that our former selves are the enemy to the desired self that we want to become.

Everyday we must commit our selves mentally never to enter a place of complacency. We must have a never ceasing desire in our preaching to be stretched, receive molding and mentorship beyond our current status. How often have you heard stories about preachers that were dynamic proclaimers of the gospel? These preachers were viewed as the cream of the crop and an example of how discipline preaching and a discipline lifestyle before Christ can transform into power in the preaching presentation. Now there are conversations concerning the forward direction of preaching and those preachers previously mentioned barely receive honorable mention.

Unfortunately there are preachers that just settle with getting by living on past sermon ideas and name recognition and they forget the elation in the preparation which gave them a peculiarity in their preaching. Peyton Manning of the Denver Broncos stated in a interview after being questioned about retirement prior to the Super bowl against the Seahawks if he wins would he retire. He stated that when practicing to get better stops becoming fun and the enjoyment of preparation has left then I am ready to give up the game. We must fall in love with the preparing as much as we love the proclaiming.

There is someone that is reading this that has lost your fire or the wick of desire is fluttering with a chance of going out. Make a decision today that you are going to get back to having passion for preaching and start making an even greater impact than before. God is waiting to use you mightily again open your heart to this ubiquitous usage by God. Lets start today as being a fresh chapter of your preaching ministry. I am excited for you so lets turn the page on ministry and on our lives. If you are ready to move forward then continue reading.

Questions for Reflections

What is your self-image as a man or woman of God?

How has others view of your ministry enhanced or hindered your growth?

How do you think God views your ministry?

What steps will you implement to assure that you keep a healthy view of yourself and your ministry?

Ministry can be fruitful only if it grows out of a direct and intimate encounter with our Lord.

Mother Teresa

Determining your Paradigm of Preaching

Chapter 2

As we begin this chapter on the paradigm of preaching I believe it would be best if we explore a working definition of what preaching can be defined as. Several preaching professors, scholars and wizards of homiletics have given their contribution of a working definition of what this business of preaching is about. Here are some of their insights:

Gardner Calvin Taylor says that Preaching is the communication of truth by man to men. It has in it two essential elements truth and personality. Neither of those can it spare and still be preaching. (Taylor 1977,25)

Charles Koller offers the insight that Preaching is personal witnessing with the aim of communicating faith and conviction (Koller 1962, 17)

Samuel Dewitt Proctor suggest that preaching is not recitation or is declamation; It is a proclamation, alive and touched with the finger of God. (Proctor 1994, 9)

Paul Wilson views preaching as follows; The central purpose of preaching is the disclosure of God, an encounter with God through the Word, more than information about God. (Wilson 1995, 20).

Fred Craddock articulated Preaching is the concerted engagement of one's faculties of body, mind, and spirit. It is, then, skilled activity. But preaching has to do with a particular content, a certain message conveyed. (Preaching page 17 ipad app in kindle). These are just a couple of informative views of preaching that shape our understanding. (Craddock 2010, 17)

Preaching in my personal view is a celestial transaction that transpires through an appointed and anointed communicator (preacher) across the channel of communication from Creator, which is God to Creation, which is humanity. There must be a premise that we start from if we are going to accurately apply ourselves to the task of preaching knowing that there will be variation in our linguistic description which is ok because there is no concretized definition for preaching; Yet and still we have to acknowledge that preaching is a God ordain transaction according to the scriptures for his people to hear from him - Romans 10:14 NRSV.

Upfront work Preparing for the Preaching Pilgrimage

Now that we have defined preaching the next progression we need to consider is understanding the working definitions of the terms in the field of preaching. It would do a preacher well to acquaint ones self with the terms that they will frequently run across while learning more about the art and science of preaching. This will alleviate the frustration of frequently having to pause in study to look up terms frequently used in the field of homiletics. A book that I would recommend to begin this process is John S. McClure's book *Preaching Words 144 key Terms in Homiletics*. We need to know words such as text/pericope; expository; rhetoric; textual criticism; historical criticism; homily; proclamation; theology; philosophy; soteriology etc. There are other books for defining these terms but this particular text is a concise piece of work that will allow you to enter into the world of homiletics without a tumultuous affect.

After we have taken out the time to do some research on homiletic language and we have a basic understanding of what preaching entails we can begin to formulate a library of the necessary books to help us further our understanding. I remember reading a homileticians work on the importance of resources on one occasion that stated there aren't better sermons there are just better libraries. So if you are attempting to be effective in this business of preaching you must make the investment to get you some books that will stretch your mind theologically; that will enlighten your thoughts; and that will force you to think critically and theologically about what you will decide to stand on as your convictions concerning Jesus Christ. Next I want to briefly walk through a short list of items we need to use for the studying process

Bible: When one prepares themselves to preach every preacher needs to have a Study Bible in a word for word translation. I advise you to invest in an interlinear bible for the new and old testament. This will help with a basic understanding of a word for translating from

Greek to English or Hebrew to English. Another type of bible that's a necessity is the parallel bible. Find as many translations possible so as to familiarize yourself with the variations of the translations (we will revisit the importance of that later.) The final thing you will need is a Life Application Bible. This bible should have the necessary elements needed to brew over scripture with a critical eye to discover details that would be otherwise missed if it just had a translation that did not have any introductory material to the book or concise commentary concerning the verses and footnotes to illuminate things such as customs or variations to a word. These sources can be found in Logos, Word Search or Bible apps.

Dictionaries and Thesaurus: Another source that is important to the preparation process is a Bible Dictionary. You will need to purchase a dictionary that is not dated but accurate in its meanings. One in particular is the Holman's Bible Dictionary. This dictionary focuses on the meanings of names, places and terms used in the bible. You will also need a English dictionary. This dictionary will be used in order to give you quick and easy ways to define the words you do not know. *Please do not make the mistake of using this dictionary to look up bible terms because in Hebrew and Greek, meanings can be different from English.* The last thing that you need is a Thesaurus, this will allow for you to receive help in creating alliterative points that have the same letter or to formulate runs which I will discuss in the chapters to come. You should never come across a word that lacks familiarity and not stop and take time to research it. Gardner

Taylor says that all we have is the Native Language and our integrity of soul while preaching.

Biblical Scholarly Works: The preacher would do well to have scholarly works as study aids to give homiletic accuracy such as Bible Dictionaries, up-to-date Commentaries, Word study tools and helps for original languages such as Hebrew, Greek, Aramaic, Introduction to Bible or various books and Survey of the Old and New Testament. All of these materials listed are a part of extensive list of the Scholarly materials you can purchase to make sure that you are not acquiring books that you will quickly matriculate from.

Study Sermons and Delivery: As a Preacher you need to become a student of preaching. There are so many great orators in history whose words have been recorded on paper or in digital form. The preacher must take time to examine technique, patterns of how a preacher connects with the people through their homiletic skill and gift. The purpose of this is to expand the preacher's mind and to do this you have to invest your mind and educate yourself on the different cultures, ethnicities, denominations, and cross gender to see what they've contributed to the body of learning that you've been exposed to on that particular topic. Albert Einstein suggested when the human mind has been stretched it does not return to its normal size.

After we have the tools to work with now you are ready to begin the process of getting into a study regiment. There must be an embracing of the privilege to daily visit the fountain of knowledge wherein we can drink of its quenching waters of theological reflection before God in arduous study. We need to establish as preachers the appointed time per day that we will study and commit to that time without undermining it with futile preoccupation.

The first Step to effective sermon preparation:

The focus on the Structure of the Sermon is the first priority which leads to crafting a Impactful message. While teaching in the seminary on the proper homiletical process needed to form quality sermons, I always initially give emphasis to the structure of the sermon. I believe that the sermons structure is the most vital part of creating a sermon. If the structure of the sermon is flimsy, weak and carelessly put together then the information collected has no synchronized way of being communicated. Therefore if the material has no proper footing or flow then it will make no sense to the congregation or audience you're trying to present it to, it becomes too tough to follow. So, we cannot skip over the structure of the sermon or short cut the process to get around it or we will find ourselves going through homiletic gymnastics to prove the point that we are trying to make in the sermon. Several preachers struggle to mature in their preaching because they aren't intentional in working on particular areas of their presentation. The main area of emphasis should be to strengthen the structure that will hold together everything else. Many delineate this as being the skeleton of the sermon.

Sermonic Structure must be prioritized

The structure is what holds the argument together in a sermon and if the foundation is weak the sermon will lose its aim and effectiveness. This reminds me of a greeting I discovered in our

ATS Magazine where Dr. Schultz spoke about the importance of foundations. Shultz mentioned that herculean feat of building Burj Khalifa in Bubai which is an impressive 2,717 feet in height twice the size of the Empire state building. But he delineated what was most impressive was the foundation. Extending 164 feet deep under the Burj Kalifa lies 58,900 cubic yards of concrete weighing over 120,000 tons. It took a year for the workers to dig deep enough and then place this foundation.

As important as the foundation is to holding up the building in Burj Khalifa when we are creating sermons to persuade those to accept our Savior Jesus Christ we need structure to make sure that we communicate concerning the cross with clarity. I believe as we are engaging in preaching for us to be consistently effective we need to have a stalwart structure that is very focused and clarion in its aim. Preaching is a powerful weapon we've been gifted with by God if used correctly. I believe that when you preach there should be a sniper rifle approach. With the sniper rifle, this particular fire arm concentrates on one target oppose to a sawed off rifle that shoots and spreads bullets everywhere. When preachers refuse to preach without structure it is liken to that sawed off shot gun approach, you will be all over the place. But, when you have structure it is just like a sniper who has a clean target to shoot at. We want to use that structure and maximize the one passage we have read to the congregation. According to Massey a Biologist C.M. Child once wrote. Structure and Function are mutually related.

There is a theory that I've been wrestling with concerning the structure of the sermon and how I can express the ideal of its importance. I have used this paradigm in class but have not yet given it a written public debut until now. I view the sermon as a wooden bridge. On this bridge there are three main wooden beams, post or legs that hold the bridge up. The legs represent the points in the sermon and the supporting structure of a sermonic presentation. It is my theory that while creating a sermon if anyone of the beams collapse because of the lack of effort to perform effective exegesis than people can't cross over to the other side of enlightenment which is just on the other side of confusion. So, it is vitally important that every point is given thorough theological consideration and time so that the bridge can land them safely to a clear understanding of the heart and word of God.

Now that we have laid the ground work for the vital things we'll need cognitively for sermonic preparation, in the following chapters I will provide a Monday through Saturday methodology which will help you prepare with more frequency and accuracy. You have come a long way and we have digested a lot but the fun is just beginning. Turn the page and let's go into the laboratory and start crafting a sermon of inspiration I can hardly wait for you to see what God is about to bring forth from your hand by using easy put together methods to create something powerful utilizing your own creativity. Let's do it!

Questions for Reflections

What comes to mind when you hear the word preaching?

Who has influenced your preaching the most currently?

How much time will you allocate for sermon preparation?

What is one schedule change that you will commit to in order to give more time to sermon prep?

"Study the text not only as a good scholar
but also as an honest struggler"
Larry Crabb

Developing Original thought in Sermon Preparation

Chapter 3

As clergy concentrate on the elements of sermon development he or she needs to give attention to methodology. The method which is used for sermonic preparation will determine the outcome of the presentation. There are preachers who use particular methods in their sermons who are oblivious to the theological terms that have been ascribed to each moment but it is executed in a correct manner. Initially, this for clergy can be flattering since they have not gone through formal education but have the technique. On the other hand, this can be very scary because if you do not arrive at a place with intentionality then what is the guarantee that you will do it with consistency. It is likened unto those who speak the English language according to Andrea Lunsford in her book *Everyday Writer*. "The grammar of our first language comes to us almost automatically without thinking much about it or even being aware of it; on the contrary tothe previous statement, we cannot carry out grammatical accuracy if we do notunderstand the proper placing of the eight parts of speech such as nouns, conjunctions, verbs, adverbs, interjections, pronouns, adjectives and prepositions. (Lunsford 2001 196)

Apologetic Argument

It is vastly important that we do what we do; know what we are doing; then be able with precision to do what we do in sermonic development. This is what I want to articulate as the apologetic argument. Apologetics in the New Testament comprises a study of the art of persuasion employed by the early Christians. The context is among the Jewish and Hellenistic thought and laid a foundation for the 2nd century apologists. (Anchor Bible Dictionary 1992, 302) In my seminary experience we called Apologetics simply the defense of the faith. I know there is much more to Apologetics but for our purposes this is enough for you to grasp as the rational for its usage.

When Sermonic crafting is taking place one has their apologetic argument. This argument will be presented to a designated audience and it is essential that the message get through to the hearer with clarity and alleviate as much ambiguity as possible. In order to project the message the inception of it must come from a solid place. I prefer the ancient methodology that was used in antiquity to prove ones case. There were a variety of concepts that were used in what they called Rhetoric used by the rhetorician.

Rhetoric - there are six major parts to rhetoric and they are as follows:

1. Exordium, or introduction, striving for attention and goodwill;
2. Narratio, describing the background of the cause;
3. Propositio, setting forth the propositions to be developed;

4. Probatio, or the main body, confirming the propositions through argumentation

5. Refutatio, disproving the propositions of the opposition; and

6. Peroratio, or conclusion, summarizing the argumentation and appealing to the audience's emotion.

This was the methodology used in order to pierce the minds of others through argumentation to convince an individual through persuasion. In contemporary times we focus our attention mainly on the proposition in the preparation of the oratorical presentation. Samuel Proctor also wrote about this influence on preaching from rhetoricians when he stated: Students of philosophy will recognize this method as the dialect found in the writings of George Wilhelmina Friedrich Hegell 1770-1831. This dialectical approach to the search for truth was also found in the writings of Empedocles in the fifth century B.C.E. in Aristotle's idea of the golden mean (Proctor 1994, 29)

The proposition is what I refer to as the heartbeat of the sermon. The proposition is the nucleus or center of life of a sermon. It is the steering wheel so to speak of the salvific vehicle that you are using to carry sinners from their transgression to the saving knowledge of Jesus Christ. Without the steering wheel on an automobile the vehicle lacks direction and that is the same if the sermon lacks a proposition, the preacher lacks focus as to where they are going. The sermon that a person is preaching as Proctor profoundly says should be able to be stated in one sentence or at most two. If the proposition does not encapsulate the entire sermon in those sentences then a preacher is not ready to preach this sermon because they cannot fully understand the angle of the passage they have selected.

In my experience during a homiletics class, Dr. Branch and Dr. Nelson taught us that the proposition is the burning sensation in the preacher concerning a subject matter that they have to preach due to a problem which needs addressing. Enveloped within this process are two important concepts which are derived from the proposition which are the thesis and the antithesis. It is between these two concepts that something is delineated as the tension established in the text. This is when the antithesis is pushing against the thesis, not for controversy but it allows us the ability and opportunity to engage in problem solving in preaching. When preaching is presented in this matter it will keep the audience intrigued and they will continue the journey with you throughout the presentation. First we will examine the thesis of the text.

Thesis

The Thesis is the sermons main idea. Samuel Proctor called the thesis the original purpose, expanded and clearly stated. (Proctor 1994, 73) The thesis can be viewed also as the undergirding thematic thrust of the sermon used! Clergy must carefully select the thesis because it is not excavated from your own opinion of what the text should say. This concept should be derived from the text itself. Clergy should echo the sound the text has already said. An echo of any sound is not derived from a different source it comes from the original sound and it projects further through faint repetition. In a sense the clergies responsibility is to echo the text with clarity for people to understand the original sound in a contemporary ecclesiastical setting. There must be a dissuading of creating our own sound and forcing the text to echo what we want to say oppose to what the Lord has already said.

Haddon Robinson, in his book *Biblical Preaching, when talking* about the thesis of a sermon describes this as the importance of a single idea. He stated:

> **Students of public speaking and preaching have argued for centuries that effective communication demands a single theme. Rhetoricians hold to this so strongly that virtually every textbook devotes space to a treatment of the principle. Terminology may vary – central idea, proposition, theme, thesis statement, main thought- but the concept is the same: an effective speech "centers on one specific thing a central idea. (Robinson 2001, 36)**

Antithesis

The Antithesis is the opposite of the Thesis. For example, if you say the thesis is cold then the Antithesis is hot; if you say the thesis is sunshine then the antithesis is a storm; if you say that the thesis is good then the antithesis is bad;if you say the thesis is hate then the antithesis would be love. Whatever that which diametrically opposes the thesis that is the antithesis. Normally I advise for those who are preaching to initialize the sermon with antithetical language in the

introduction. The reason why I believe this is important   s'

people unfortunately are more apt to listen to the negati   I

the positive. If you begin with this and this is psychologic: r

the people are it is easier to keep the sermonic train on t   i

in their mind but if you start with sunshine and glitz an   (

they may get derailed and believe that you can't relate to r((

issues which makes your presentation irrelevant. I heard D

Thomas say that the truth is always relevant. (C.L. Frankl

of a prophet conference April 25) The question is how h

we package that truth in order that the people that receiv

mentally, and spiritually nourished by the truth they recei

will return to these concepts later in the book to clarify the u:

them in the sermon.

Original Thought

After you have done your research and homework concernin

original context of the text and you've consulted scholarly sou

then you can offer an original thought in the sermon. In my Do

of Ministry program at Ashland Seminary we were notified that

have to collect the voices of others initially. Beginning at chap

one you have the introduction and rationale, the second chap

which was the biblical, theological and historical view of the proje(

chapter three was the review of the literature, chapter four is tl

methodology, chapter five was reporting the results, and the fin:

chapter were my reflections and implications. In every chapter prio

to my final chapter I had to collect the voices of the scholars through

research. The idea was that I could not be qualified to speak on a

ibject matter as a expert if there was a failure to collect the voices. was in chapter 6 that I could give my hermeneutic to my subject matter which was validated because of the scholars, statistic and materials that I studied which gave me a foundation toward my original thought. I believe that this process is liken unto sermonic crafting. Before you can begin having original thoughts and creativity you can't ignore the contributions of the church fathers. It should be impossible for a preacher to ignore the value contributions given by Paul Tillich and John Calvin, or Josephus and Philo. I encourage you to read these sources prior to making dogmatic assumptions which have no true foundation in the systematic thought from the 1st century church until the present.

When I speak of original thought I am not speaking of reinventing a text but in order for you to use a hermeneutic that is accurate but yet innovative you must use your autonomy to explain the gospel in a way that no one else can. This is what I call original thought not that the content is new but the way in which it is packaged is peculiarly used through the personality of the proclaimer which offers another view of the cross. This is exciting to hear and experience for the saints of God. These original thoughts render an ineffable freshness that faintly flows over the soul and fanatically changes lives forever.

Developing the Structure – Through my studies and opportunities to teach in various seminaries and bible colleges, I have found my own personal process in which I create sermons because of what I gleaned from the opulent knowledge of others. In

later chapters, the structure that I will demonstrate there will be seen and will clearly demonstrate the process of how you can personally use these concepts

Investigation- The first responsibility that we have is investigation. In that timeless treasure, *The Elements of Biblical Exegesis* by Michael Gorman, Gorman explains that the exegetes' (the one doing the exegesis) responsibility is one and the same as the reporter who knows who to research for the dynamic details and who receives quality material through asking the right questions. He mentions the importance of the childhood questions of SQ3R There are pertinent questions that every text need to answer which helps reveal to you the meaning of a text.

Explanation- The second step in the process is that you must thoroughly (and I mean thoroughly) explain what you've just investigated in concise form of communication. The explanation of the research must bring the material back to life. The preacher must make the sermon a living organism which people can interact with and feel. This is so they may experience the living Christ through the living organism of his word through sermonic form.

Illustration- The third step is the use of stories be it bible stories or personal experiences. I am an advocate for keeping your mind focused on preaching so that the Lord will allow you to ease drop on the very things in your midst daily which we tend to miss so that you can gain a clearer understanding through life experience. I agree that there is preaching everywhere except in the mind of those who are not intentional in their pursuit of God talk. In order for preachers homiletic radar to pick up on life changing pictorials of providences portraits of love they must persistently ponder on new ways to illustrate his reconciliation to the world.

Application- The fourth element is the application. The application is the so what of the process. During the investigation process leading to explanation and even with a great illustration the question is what should the person take away. If there is no transferrable principles or what we Pastor's call marching orders given to allow your theology to transfer into the practical everyday life all of this technique is pointless. We must deliver the people the goods. Congregants come to worship to receive the compass of compassion on their course of life as they remain curious of the forth coming climate and we must give them the righteous yet responsible reply as to how to be proactive and how they should respond to their challenges.

Manifestation- The fifth step is the manifestation. In this section how does the take away in application impact those in whom they are connected to? After you have instructed them in the word on how they should address circumstances how does this liberation translate in the effectuation of impact in the life of the body of Christ. How will God use them today to be a catalyst and a game changer because of the message that has been heeded?

Questions for Reflections

According to the reading how important is the proposition to the process of preaching?

What is your method for exegesis?

Are you willing to veer from your former method if a better one is presented?

How can you immediately implement these changes in your preaching?

I have seen words in sentences, I have seen words misspelled,

I have seen words misinterpreted but on Calvary this was

the first time I ever saw a word bleed. When you preach

do we see the Word bleeding for our salvation?

- Rev. Joseph Chapman

Day One acquainting yourself with the Text

Chapter 4

The first step that we should consider making is preparing a fertile ground for sermon development. It is not sufficient enough to just open a Bible and begin crafting a sermon we need to have an appointed time and an appointed place that we study the word of God. We need to consecrate these moments so that we develop the connections with these eternal words translated through servant personalities to earthlings that are attempting to escape the erosion of their notorious nature.

I believe that there is a rhythm to studying, that there is a zone of meditation so to speak where you can get a great deal accomplished but you must find and guard that sacred space. When you have found that place of comfort and serenity for the work of God then sanctify the place and mark it as a place of spiritual oasis for your soul.

Paul informs Timothy in 2Timothy 2:15 NRSV to study to show yourself approved before God a workman that need not to be ashamed rightly dividing the word of truth. The word rightly divide in the Greek is orthotomeiv in the transliteration which is a compound verb: temeiv "to cut" and orthos "straight" when you put it together it means to cut a straight path. We are to prepare ourselves to give it to the people straight. It was stated best by that legend of preaching Fred Craddock that Studying is an act of obedience: "You shall love the Lord your God with all of your mind." It is a time of Worship: An hour at study said the rabbis, is in the sight of the Holy One, Blessed be He, as an hour of prayer." What minister has not experienced a desk becoming an altar?

As you consider the task before you of sermon development you must decide what day will be my own personal starting point. Will you begin on Sunday or Monday etc... When you select the day that you will begin, the preparation process, you must commit yourself to that day and don't compromise. If you compromise the initial day of sermon development the days will begin to fall like dominos therefore you must guard that initial day. If you discipline yourself for that one day than other days, weeks and years of discipline will follow. After the study day has been selected now you must choose the time and be sure that the time selected works best for you.

I am programmed to rise early in the morning approximately 4:00 am is my peak thinking time. It is quiet in my home and parishioner's calls are seldom at that hour. Now let me impress upon you that this is how my mind and body is programmed yours may not be programmed the same way but as long as you have uninterrupted time with God in study you can select what works best for you. Rick Warren on a You Tube video explained that a lot of us get caught up in time management when we should emphasize energy management. What is the best time for thinking and what is the best time to work with your hands. Only you know how you're programmed so select wisely and police your own schedule to make sure you follow through.

Another great investment is putting a preaching plan in place in order to desist from having to search for a text to preach. Stephen Rummage has a wonderful book on planning your preaching which will guide you towards a strategic methodological approach to your sermon selection for the year or beyond.

Investigation

Following your selection of the text the initial step is to investigate the book of the bible thoroughly. The exergete needs to search a text out through text such as the *Survey of the Old or New Testament* depending on the scripture selected. Also, you should seek scholarly sources on the background of that particular book to consult. During the time in which you are doing this research you should take accurate notes of the important points that you have read. You should not just rewrite what the text is saying in these sources (you already have the book!), you need to capture a snap shot of information and document it so well that you can return to it and know how to insert it into the proper place in your sermon. This means that we are introducing those scholars on our terms and using the information that they have in order to support our proposition. Also please write a note of where you receive the quote in order to give the proper credit for the idea. When you quote individuals in your sermon this does not take away from the sermon it adds to the credibility of the preacher. This means that we are bringing those scholars on our terms and using the information that they have in order to support our proposition.

There are two other sources that will benefit you in your research of passages and they are an extensive Bible Dictionary that has several volumes and an Encyclopedia of the Bible. These sources will give you invaluable information for homilitical use. In addition these text are often accompanied with strong bibliographies to which you should research further on the passage selected. I must warn you that when you initially preach out of a particular book of the bible you'll need to research it as thoroughly as possible with quality sources. If the exergete does their due diligence they will not have to continue repeating this same step every time they preach out of that particular book they've researched.

The reason that you should take the time and engage this process is because you are building your own commentary so to speak that you can depend on and is now at your finger tips. This will give you more time in the future to work on exergesis oppose to having your time consumed with researching the historical facts unless you are opposed to books that you have not yet read.

This investigation process helps us to invest in building our Hermeneutic. Hermeneutic, to give a concise definition is the art and science of interpretation. According to Grant Osborne in his book *The Hermeneutical Spiral* he speaks of the text and context: as spheres that actually intersect one another. There are three levels in his philosophy: exegesis, devotional, and sermonic. In the exegesis is the original meaning (original audience); devotional means what does it mean to me (personally); the third element is sermonic how will this be shared with others after it has impacted me personally. "Only a carefully defined hermeneutic can keep one wedded to the text". (Osborne 1991, 7)

There are several concepts that you should be hermeneutically sensitive to while taking notes and studying the background of these sacred text. What are the key dates in the life of the book? Who is the author(s) if it is known? Who are the significant leaders of the book? What events have shaped the importance of this book? Research the pattern of the authors themes that reoccur often so you can see the book from the author's world view. The exegete also would do well to find books that are wrote exclusively on their book of the Bible. These text offer more of a concentration and depth of information than even the several volume set commentaries on different passages.

Now that you have done the background work on the book, take out the time and read the entire book in one seating. While you are reading the book, make side notes noting extensively those things that greatly intrigue you. You will need to read this book all the way through because you will need to experience the shifts in the text and the repetition that is used in the text that you are reading. After you read the text through, this is the time to draft in your note book an outline of the entire book for your own purposes. Try to resist the temptation to use the outline that is provided by the Life Application Bible or Commentaries, we are trying to remain open to original thought. That concept is very important, original thought is what allows your mind to push itself to It's theological limits so that you can continue growing in grace.

As a biblical based preacher there should be an acknowledgement that a voracious amount of reading is going to be necessary. In the words of Augustine in The Confessions 8.12 after hearing a child at play he stated "Take up and read, take up and read." (Gorman 2009, 9) I encourage you to continue reading even when some text yield us a modicum of insight. There are times when the small insights and ideas that we receive will give birth to other ideas and will grow into a vibrant thought provoking idea that'll make a difference in the transition of a message to give a waiting congregant the ah ha moment in their lives. You must keep reminding yourself that a little reading brings limitation to how you can articulate what you desire to convey to the readers and listeners.

Here is an example of the outline in which I am speaking of:

The Book of Jonah

   I. Jonah's original call from God

   A. Dialogue with Jonah

   B. Directive given to Jonah

   C. Disobedience of Jonah

   D. Digesting of Jonah by the Great Fish

   II. Jonah's petition from the Belly

   A. Hope while in the belly

   B. Horrific view from the belly

   C. Help acknowledged while in the belly

III. Jonah's second call to Nineveh

A. Awaken of the Nineveh assignment

B. Arrival of Jonah in Nineveh

C. Acceptance of God from the People of Nineveh

IV. Jonah's anger toward Nineveh's Repentance

A. Displeasure concerning the Nineveh Dilemma

B. Disappointment in the anger of Jonah

C. Distress over the withering of the Bush

D. Disposition of Jonah for the people

Following the completion of the outline we are now ready to go to our text and continue the investigation process. Take the selected text that you have and read it twenty-five times (literally) in the version of the Bible you will be preaching from. This process is used to download this scripture into the ponderings of your mind but also to allow the scripture to saturate your spirit. Following this you should write the text out in your own words so that it becomes easier for you to remember and this will also let you know that you know the story completely which makes it easier to transition in the preaching moment. (Don't be afraid to read this out loud so that you are downloading it into your subconscious).

Please note in your notebook that you should write these things in a organized fashion so that you can continue to build on the sermon in every preparatory moment. If you are not organized then you will become overwhelmed and make for yourself twice the work.

Your text has been selected you have read over it in depth the third step is that you need to search out as many versions of the Bible as possible on your particular text. The parallel bible would be a good resource to start with. While reading the other various translations have your preselected text next to you so that you can document the variances in the text. This documentation will become useful for crafting which selection of words you will desire to use while preaching this text, for example:

Psalm 30:5b

KJV Weeping may endure for a night but joy cometh in the morning

NRSV Weeping may linger for the night, but joy comes with the morning.

MSG The nights of crying your eyes out give way to days of laughter

ESV Weeping may tarry for the night but joy comes with the morning

After experiencing these translations your public text you've decided to read may change but it doesn't mean that the exegesis process will change. There can be one word that makes the difference in driving home the point that you want to make in a sermonic presentation. One practice we want to avoid is "proofing text, this is when a doctrine or practice merely alludes to a text without considering its original inspired meaning". (Osborne 1991,7) Taking the time and reading these different versions of a particular pericope can be used to ones advantage to tell the congregants the different options than expose the one you desire most and explain why to nail the point home in your sermon.

Biblical Brainstorming

Now that you have taken the time to research a particular section in the background of the book which bares your scripture transition, it is time to learn how to make educated guess concerning possible points and observations from your text. The method of Selah as Caesar Clark would say is very important. You'll need to pause and reflect on the lesson from the original audience and determine how it affects the present audience. Follow the text closely and write down those initial thoughts that leap with luster from the pages for you. Only a carefully defined hermeneutic can keep one wedded to the text. Don't give way to hesitancy in this experience. No answer is a stupid answer these initial observations will be refined and revised as the sermon continues to take on its own life but for now you need to get your sermonic juices flowing.

This process is like stretching before a rigorous activity or like warming up prior to the main event. We have to take time and allow for our theological precision to warm up. We have to engage in what Samuel Proctor calls a tabula rasa so that you can prepare to receive what the Lord is birthing in your spirit.

Buddying with others Biblically

Earlier in the book I spoke about how important partnerships are in ministry. You need to surround yourself with preachers who are serious, sincere, scripturally rooted and able to freely stretch your initial thoughts through critique before you find yourself in the great abyss theologically and you are daring to preach something that has no foundation dating back to the church fathers.

Having this inner circle of preachers around you will allow for you to express your ideas audibly. Sometimes we just need to have the opportunity to hear our theological thoughts out loud in order that they may be challenged and later refined. Also as we are expressing our ideas to others, ideas begin to come. As we are expressing the original ideas write them down for later consideration. The third dimension to this dialogue is that your buddy in ministry will be able to give you some advice on the direction you could possibly venture into or just say something to trigger the idea that you were missing to make your direction more clarion for communicating. I believe that it is healthy to once a week share with others your theological thoughts. When you share these thoughts this allows for you to process the text and remember it through repetition. In preaching we possess theological muscles and our desire is for those muscles to grow but the only way this can happen is by exercising in dialogue our theology.

These experiences with your buddies will prove to be moments of inspiration but also moments of encouragement. This is another form of studying because when you are engaged in biblical dialogue concerning a text, through brainstorming it willreveal to you if you can explain it and if you can explain it you certainly can preach it!

I can truly say that I have been blessed with a diversity of preachers that I can call, from my mentors, to students that have just began their PhD programs, to individuals that have an opulence of observation for scripture who have not entered the corridors of theological institutions. These individuals through the years have willed their way to an outstanding oasis of insight. Through the years, these dialogues have allowed me to learn from others all while allowing me to hear my own homiletical heartbeat. This exercise can be fulfilling and freeing to the mind. There are those who oppose such a practice and they become islands to themselves and unfortunately are found at a loss because there's always someone that you can learn from who and can stretch your shrunken prospective but you have to be open to the possibilities. You are Paul Tillch's five minute theologian. There is a theologian in all of us crying from the wilderness of creativity to share with others so lets do it!

Questions and Reflections

Do you have a sacred space for preparation? If not, what area are you willing to designate?

What type of questions should you ask the text?

What source outside of the bible will you purchase to enhance your moments of preparation?

A talk (sermon) is a voyage. It must be charted. The speaker
(Preacher) who starts nowhere usually gets there.

–Dale Carnegie

Day Two Starting to Build the Bridge

Chapter 5

In my theological framework I view sermons as a journey. The journey begins when God pulls up to the ecclesiastical curb of your existence and has the Holy Spirit blow open the door with his peerless pnema and tells you hop in let's take a ride. You are not in the drivers seat God is which means he is in control of where we are going and we are going where God is going. When we attempt to construct sermons we should be going where God is going or better yet where God has already been!

During my beginning stage of learning sermon structure my beloved Pastor referred me to a book that I have been reading and teaching from for the past sixteen years -. Charles Koller's book *How to Preach Without Notes*. A lot of people avoid this book if they believe that they'll never preach without a manuscript but when reading this text you see how Koller makes a case for why you should preach without manuscript with his ultimate goal being the structure of the sermon. For the second day of sermon preparation, I adapted Charles Koller's investigative style.

Focusing on the Fragments

I believe when we approach a text there are some that become intimidating to us. This happens especially when we look at Old Testament passages that span several chapters. There is no need for us to be rattled by those lengthy text we just need a methodology that we can use to capture what the creator put in our gut. When we are viewing scripture we need to have a focus liken to that sniper I spoke of earlier in the introduction and we need one target. The topic of selection doesn't need to be too broad We need to implement Koller's method of questioning the text to allow us to focus on the fragments of the text.

There are six questions that we should be focused on: Who, What, When, Where, How, and Why? If we answer these questions we have a good sense of the tools that we have at our disposal as we paint the master piece. I look at this method as being analogous to forming a large homilitical puzzle. We have all the pieces we need through this paradigm of study, we just need to put them in the right place for the people to see the big picture.

We will use John 3:16 for our example

Who? We need to identify in the text the pronouns and the nouns

What? This question concentrates on what happen in the text.

When? There must be caution with this question because it is twofold. "When" deals with a state of time or chronology. It also deals with the phrase when you do this then this will happen

Where? "Where" focuses on the place where the activity transpires. It can be a place or a state of being

Why? This question gives emphasis on why was it done in the text and what was the reasoning or rational

How? "How" is based on how do we get this done. This question is usually where we get the marching orders or the formula to get things done - this is how we do it.

John 3:16: For God so love the World that he gave his only begotten son that whosoever believeth in him should not parish but have everlasting life.

Who?	What?	When?	Where?	How?	Why?
God	Loved	Believeth	World	Love	Not perish
World	Gave		In Him	Gave	Love
His	Only			Believeth	Everlasting-life
Son	Believeth			In him	
Whosoever	Perish				
Him	Everlasting-Life				

From these Focused Fragments this is where you will derive a proposition which guides the sermon. By the second day of sermon prep you should have a proposition. We can't craft any points from a particular angle if we don't have a proposition. I believe this is a good time to mention that when we are coming up with our proposition we must allow for it to be birthed from the text. Preach what you read and not what you hear. The scriptures are inexhaustible and has the depth that one can never reach the bottom therefore, be accurate yet creative. This process is exegesis. Gorman classifies exegesis as coming from the technique verb exegeisthai meaning to lead out (ex, "out" + hegeisthai, "to lead"). (Gorman 2009, 10)

Ask yourself which angle I desire to preach this passage: This exercise always keeps your preaching fresh and invigorating.

God's view
Sinners view
Son's view

Let's take it from God's angle where the sermon would be based on his participation with humanity.

Proposition: <u>Providence</u> gives <u>Provision</u> through his <u>Passionate Participation</u>

(God)   (Gave)   (so love)

Now that I have a proposition I can guide my points based on the steering of my proposition.

Who?	What?	When?	Where?	How?	Why?
God-I. Super natural Source World- II. Saturated with Sin His Son- III. Spotless Savior Whosoever-IV. Sacredly Selected	Loved Gave Only Believeth Perish Everlasting-Life	Believeth	World In Him	Love Gave Believeth In him	Not perish Love Everlasting-life

I.   **Supernatural Source**

II. **Saturated with Sin**

III. **Spotless Savior**

IV. **Sacredly Selected**

Proposition: <u>Providence</u> gives <u>Provision</u> through his <u>Passionate</u> <u>Participation</u>

By day two you should have an underdeveloped skeleton that you can work with and grow it from fragments into a full body sermon. This process takes some work so don't underestimate the process of sermon development it takes some time but if you continue using the methodology it becomes less challenging as time goes on.

The proposition should be concise and clear you should invest enough time to add scholarship to the proposition. Do not discount the importance of this step. Your proposition should be the most emphasized phrase in your whole sermonic presentation. It will afford you to remain on track and it will remind the audience where you are taking them on the journey.

Articulating and identifying the Antithesis and Thesis

After you've dropped anchor on your proposition the next step in the process is that you'll need to create a thesis statement from the proposition. Samuel Proctor explained that the sermon is launched by a clear presentation of a strong antithesis, but it is propelled by the thesis which is the proposition, the original purpose expanded and clearly stated.

The Antithesis is the problem that is in need of a solution. Dr. Nelson used to tell us that we needed to ask ourselves what is burning in me that says this is why I have been arrested and pushed by the problem to preach this. I believe it is the noise that needs to be quieted; the injustices as King said has been miscarried and need to have a redivivus, it is the oppression that needs to be satisfied with clinching courageous bells of freedom. You must have an arresting "why" to preach this word.

The Antithesis is the issue that you believe is worthy to be raised in order to change the lives of the people in the pulpit and the pews. This would be simply thought as the opposite of the thesis. After explaining the thesis I will give a few examples.

The Thesis is the one statement that gives direction to the entire sermon, it is very closely knit to the proposition. The Thesis also can be delineated as the central idea of your topic. Joan Detz enlightens us on the power of precision of a thesis by saying it assist us in limiting our focus and organizing our material around a central idea. **(Detz 42, 2014) Earlier I stated that the proposition is the steering wheel, the Thesis is the engine. Without the Thesis the sermon, the sermonic car can shine but can't get started on a sacred sojourn without the engine. When we identify the Thesis then the Antithesis is the opposite of it. Below you'll find Antithesis versus Thesis example:

Antithesis	Thesis
Sorrow	Joy
Up	Down
Doubt	Faith
Lack	Abundance

After we have identified both of these correctly we lean the Thesis against the Antithesis and when they push against one another this creates tension in the text. We give ambiguity and the dubious but not futile syllogisms. The thesis needs the antithesis and the antithesis needs the thesis they cannot survive exclusive from one another; it's like light and darkness they complement one another and that is the same reality with the power of Antithesis and the Thesis.

Using the Thesis or Antithesis in the introduction

I have benefited immensely when using my Antithesis in my introduction of the sermon initially opposed to the Thesis. The reason why I have frequently used the Antithesis first is that people are naturally intrigued by problems more than they are with the solutions. If you give people the solution immediately they lose interest in the whining and the weaving of the journey through

Jordanian heights and Judean costal plains of the text therefore I start with the Antithesis. Now the Thesis is good for a introduction if you have a great transition to how problems can arise and with the text you answer the problems. Now when you transition well from Thesis to Antithesis you will create the tension you need to continue a strong sermonic stride.

Tension in the Text

I became very acclimated to this expression 'tension in the text' when I heard preachers such as Bishop Noel Jones, Tolan Morgan, David Johnson, Cedric Jones, and Curtis Grant and a few other Preachers. This style really intrigued me. It was a methodology to raise problems throughout a pericope to keep people thinking with you while unveiling an oasis of revelation that were birthed through the wound of a worrisome problem.

After hearing this style of preaching, I instantly fell in love with it and begin to study every preacher and sermon that had this element as I attempted to aggressively master it. Preaching is so elusive that when you believe you are having mild success you will have sermonic slippage. The tension of the text is not trying to come up with outlandish observations that are oblivious to the text and are toxic theologically to the body. Tension in the text is not trying to stretch the triune truths of God in order to get people to shout over how clever you are with your cryptic linguistics but it is a method to shed light on what was there all the time.

This is likened to my experience at Chucky Cheese. When you enter the establishment they stamp your hand with a stamper that contains some type of liquid and then stamp your children's hands with the same. After you have been energized and entertained with all sorts of games, food and live entertainment on your way out you are met by staff holding a florescent light that reveals numbers in the stamped area. The parents number matches the number stamped on their child. It was always there but others could not see it until the designated florescent light was shined upon it. That is what the tension of the text is, shining the florescent light of glory on the text that you match the fathers will with his children's will so that the people can be counted in the number of those who might be saved!

There is one last thing that I want to speak to prior to me moving from this concept. I normally study about 4:00 a.m. when it is still yet early and the atmosphere is serene and I can privately argue with the text. It is not strange for me to hear my self asking the text questions. Why this; Why did the Lord do this; How did this happen; If it is like this then why is it like that? When I go to the Bible I am an interrogator for truth!

I am an anointed apologist that pushes and pulls the text because I know through the test of time that the text has been tested and is true and if you use it wisely and come before it humble it will yield you the answers you seek or give you the comfort that God alone knows. If you are going to learn this style you have to ask the right questions not just any questions. You have to discipline yourself not to take the easy surface point but to struggle with the text as Jacob wrestled with the Angel knowing that God really wants you to prevail so that you can receive transformation in your thoughts and soul.

There are several preachers that retreat from a text because the insight does not come instantly. Some of the best sermons that I have preached were from passages that made we scratch my head and made me feel like I would never get to a sermon that was strong substantively. Success comes through the struggle of chipping away at the rock of the text. Liken to Michelangelo you don't see a rock you see the statue within the rock and you have to usher it into reality. Often times struggle is necessary to preach passages with conviction and power!

Questions and Reflections

What is the importance of an effective sermon?

How are people immediately affected by your preaching?

Who will be responsible to keep you accountable for your sermonic accuracy?

What makes a sermonic Master piece is not what you put in the
sermon-- it is what you strategically leave out of the sermon.

- Rev. Tellis Chapman

Day three the Meat of the Message Drafting Points

Chapter 6

On one occasion I had the pleasure of assisting as an armor bearer for the Late Albert Louis Patterson in my opinion one of the greatest expository preachers in the English speaking world! Patterson spirit was as attractive as his unexcelled eloquence. I had the opportunity to acquaint myself further with him following his ministering at the BM&E State Convention. I had an uninterrupted twenty minutes to be in the presences with this antique analytical hero whose content was more valuable then gold. I made an inquiry to Patterson: "How do you examine a text and what do you initially gaze at. Patterson responded simply match the verbs with the proper nouns in the text and you have the text. He further explained the importance of the verb is always connect to its noun.

There were other preaching pedagogical practices we spoke about which at this time I will borrow a scriptural expression of Paul; I am not able to express it after visiting the third heaven of preacher-dom with Patterson! I believe that this is a lesson within its self that there are some things you only can receive preachers when your humble enough to submit to wise counsel.

I believe that A Louis Patterson statements give us an excellent launching pad to leap into this ideal of formulating vibrant points. Patterson used the methodology of matching the nouns with the verbs to make strong sermonic points. In the text Living Water for Thirsty Soul Marvin McMickle articulates these pronouns as the leaders of the text. The leaders in the text are those who are identified as significant to the undergirding themes of the text. We are instructed by McMickle to focus our attention on what actions the characters are performing in the episodic encounter in the pericope that have been chosen. In addition to using the actions of the characters it would be advantageous to research the names and the place where he/she resided in the text. The etymological (Hebrew or Greek) of the text will cause for your point to have enough content in order to bring to life a vibrant point.

This concept of the sermonic points standing on their own alludes back to the pillars of the sermonic bridge. When you prioritize developing the strength of each point Individually then they can stand on their own. If the points initially crafted are anemic then revise the point or check the proposition to verify if the point's direction is aligned with the proposition. By now your curiosity may be heightened concerning the proper homiletic ingredients that cultivate a vibrant point?

Strong Points

A Strong sermonic point first has to be derived from exegesis. The practice of excavation is advised to discover authentic and integral meanings being drawn out of the text. I don't care how profound a point is in a sermon the question is does that point come directly from the text. Gardner Taylor says that when we bruise the text we cause bruises on the people. Taylor further says we have to find what street the text is on, what boulevards does it land on. We have to ask the text as the late Dr. Frederick G. Sampson said "who are you going to lift today or I refuse to preach you"!

A preacher will do him/herself well to preach the points in chronological order; this will make you avoid leaping over invaluable insights textually to arrive at the point that you believe is going to be the most impactful. Through ministerial experience I have learned that every congregation is different, and what allows one congregation to take hold of the message that point won't necessarily be effective in another setting! Preachers you have to stay focused and craft your points word by word phrase by phrase honor the process don't rush it. Effective sermons are saturated with points that build on each point. This assures a strong message that doesn't lean on homiletic lenses of laziness but rather sermonic points that are linked together which leads the lost to the loving knowledge of the Lord; but if the points are weak liken unto the beams under a bridge it will give way to a catastrophic collapse of condemnation.

Pastor Sandy F. Ray, who possessed influential pulpit prowess, helped pulpit prodigies in crafting points when Ray advised its liken unto going grocery shopping. His mother while going grocery shopping kept in mind that several of her children had acquiesced to certain taste that was different from the others and she would keep in mind that Sandy like this but David like that and so on. But when she returned home everyone could get something. This mindset of Ray's mother that Pastor Ray adopted for technique in sermonic discovery is profitable to us when attempting to craft great points we should allow everyone to gain something. Paul said in 1 Corinthians 9:19 NRSV "I became all things to all men (women) so that I may win some." Preachers! Let us go grocery shopping to create points that are wholesome to the soul.

In my own style of preaching I like to go after the psychological element and work my way to the emotional. I prefer to preach points from the intellectual slant and work my way down to lay terminology where everyone can grasp it. I heard a preacher say you should be so deep that adults can swim in it but so shallow that a baby can wade in the waters.

Context

When you are building your point the contextual element must hold priority. On many occasions I have experienced in Ecclesiastical gatherings preachers use Matthew 18:20 if two or three are gathering in my name I will be there in the midst and someone may craft a point "the presence of God despite numerical preference". Well this text has little to do with numeric presence it has to do with the correction of notorious sin. We must practice reading prior to our text and after the text in order that you may obtain a context. When you craft a point it needs to be contextually correct.

Also it would be beneficial to grasp an understanding of textual criticism. This will help to shape your theological views better when this text is taken apart and examine for you and allows you to see how it was viewed by church fathers etc.

Content

The next element that a point should be comprised of is the right content. Often there is a lot of information is enveloped in a point but is the information relevant and useful for the designated purpose to push the perspective of the sermon. One of the grave mistakes that has become popular for crafting points is looking up terms in the English dictionary attempting to get a biblical meaning this can cripple your point because what it means in the English my not be what it interprets in the Greek or Hebrew!

An Example of this naive observation is in the term witness in Acts chapter 2 it says that you shall be my witness some believe that this word witness is eluding to the witness stand that one stand on in court when in all actuality the Greek word is martyria which is where we get the word martyr so Jesus isn't inviting the disciples to bask in convenience of a witness stand but he is inviting them to literally come and die with him. I will speak of the importance of the correct use of Greek and Hebrew further in the next chapter.

Connections

The third element to a good point is the connections. How does this point connect initially with this verse? One thing that is too common is that preachers get a point and go and sprint to grasp connecting (supporting) scriptures oppose to giving a explanation of the scripture before them. I believe you ought to explain what you read first.

There are so many concepts, theological doctrines, translations, dates, places and events that are present that there should be a sufficient amount of information to exclusively deal with the public reading of the text. When you use supporting scripture use it as an addition to and not the main attraction or you should have used it as the preferred text and not the supportive one. It is a homiletic error to clog a sermon with a continuance line of supporting scriptures and quotes. Prior to connecting a scripture make sure you investigate the context of that text because the words may appear to fit but they do not always fit the context; never forget this phrase: Context is King or Queen and you cannot usurp it.

Compartmentalized

The fourth element is compartmentalized this means the congregant should be able to carry that point away and apply it to their lives. It is what my Pastor, Tellis Chapman, calls giving them their marching orders. This phraseology suggest that now that I have conveyed this information or bestowed this knowledge, what do we do with this information next that we have had bestowed upon us for our blessed benefit? This is where the importance of Application lay. We have to take the biblical principles and lessons and apply them to our culture and our lives. We have to make it indigenous to those who are on the pew, we have to make the word come alive to them, and not just a dry dingy document. It must come alive to them through relating the text through everyday life experience and challenges and yet remaining true to the original intent of the text.

We have an example of this in the book of Daniel where King Darius made a damnable decision and God took fingers and wrote on the wall. To get people to understand in an American cultural context, we can elude to the phenomenon of that social media site facebook which is a network that frequently connects people with present and past familiars through timelines and writing on the walls of friends. We can use this phraseology of writing on the wall as a way to remain relevant and protecting the integrity of the original audience and yet speak about how God can write on the walls of those whom he has no friend request submitted. Cannot you see how enlightening and insightful that can be to people who are being oppressed whose deposition is nihilistic and in posture of pedantic predicaments to convey to them there is hope for them if they turn from their damnable decision just as there could have been hope for Darius but if they follow the lesson it can set them free.

The final portion on the development of the points I want to allocate to making sure there is an aura of the Christ and the cross that shroud it. Whatever point you have as E.L. Branch has stated make sure that you at least have one. If you have a point it should be guided by giving men an opportunity to know Christ in his power and his might and the power of his resurrection. I refuse to craft a sermon unless I'm conscious of the Christ that can pull sinners and saints out of their crisis.

Preaching becomes hopeless and irrelevant even in what Paul calls the foolishness of preaching if there is no cross and resurrecting power to preach. This concept reminds me of my Ford Focus that I drive that has took me 200,000 miles up the highways of Ypsilanti, Ann Arbor, Ashland Ohio and so many other places to acquire my education. I yet still have that car to this day but on one occasion the car battery died from the car sitting so long without moving so I could not ignite the cars power at will. I decided to pull up my other vehicle to jump it and it took about 15 minutes but it turned over but it needed a boost to come alive.

I believe the paralyzing problem that permeates an power outage in the pulpit is that we have been settling to preach what is popular and our power has died. We need to understand to obtain our power back it only occurs when we come back in contact with the Christ and that Cross. It was the Christ event that made every wrong right; it was the Christ event that made every crooked place straighten, it was the Christ event that made every high place low. Through the shedding of his precious blood we receive power! The old wood floor church use to sing it reaches the highest mountain and it flows to the lowest valley it gives me strength from day to day and it will never lose its power!

- Andrae Crouch

Questions for Reflections

What are the dynamics of a strong sermonic point?

How do you strike a balance in the sermon through your points?

Explain the process that you will implement to create stronger points?

Day Four Refine thoughts through Commentary and Etymology Study

Chapter 7

While having the opportunity of Mentoring hundreds and instructing thousands of preachers in my Homiletics Career I have seen the impulse to run to commentaries. I want to take a moment and explain what a commentary is and what it is used for. A commentary is an analysis and interpretation of a particular text that is derived from the research of languages, context, syntax, and traditions from scholars theologians. These volumes were created to give guidance and clarity to those examining sacred text.

The question given rise is what should commentaries be used for? These sources functions are to support, and to confirm that the exegete is on track to deliver a message devoid of eisegesis. Also the commentators are trying to give information to provoke thinking not necessarily so that you can agree with them but give you the best options to interpreted the text for yourself. Commentaries are built to strengthen the argument and understanding of the person that is delivering the message.

Preachers I believe naively go directly to commentaries on day one of their sermon preparation to obtain the ideology and direction that they should drive their sermon. Unknowingly, I believe that preachers leave their own perspective in paralysis when it comes to a pericope because they look at others views and make them gospel. On the other extreme, I believe that we have preachers who never consult scholarly commentaries based upon one bad interpretation from a scholar. These preachers group all of scholars in one category because of these findings that are unbiblical and heretical but they should not be bundled with the others who have used bad theology so to speak.

There are several theories and discoveries through archaeological digs that assist in the accuracy of interpreting scripture. The majority of these scholars and theologians have given their whole existence to their lives work on a particular pericope, languages or ecclesiology! We as preachers ought to be elated that there were those that sacrificed their time, energy, and resources to give us the best possible chance to procure a precise interpretation. Commentaries I believe are gifts and not a curse to the seminarian as well as to those who have never cracked the corridors of a school as Pastor A Louis Patterson would say "The scholars help us!"

The question that might be raised by the freshly called preacher is if I just started preaching should I not go to a commentary first? The answer is absolutely not. When you are preparing a sermon you want to keep the paths of your creativity open less you experience sermonic block which is the same as writers block a lack of original ideas. It is in my observation that God has called a collection of clergy to communicate the gospel because we will have our own commentary of what we have witnessed through research and reading. Avoid making sermons that are only at best a exercise in cutting and pasting which is not an effective way to speak from the preachers heart to lost men and women. Moreover, you should collect the voices that add to the wealth of your own preaching presentation.

Adding the insight of commentaries are liken unto the entrée that is ate at a restaurant. Commentaries are the garnish and should not be the entire meal if it is then we need to just read commentaries from the pulpit or distribute copies of it through the ushers ministry while they enter in for worship.

Selecting the Best Commentary

First, I want to put out this disclaimer that I believe that commentaries are for everyone who is serious about a thorough background and interpretive understanding of scripture. That is for the child, for the teenager, for the adult congregants, for the preacher, for the professor and for the student. Based on maturity and academic training the type of commentaries that you can digest varies. Personally, I prefer to use the Word Biblical Commentary for my own background study as well as for form and explanation. Those clergy who have no theological training may not do to well reading this commentary because this commentary was written with the assumption that you have some competency with the Hebrew and Greek Language.

There are other commentaries that can fit the untrained Clergy the Believer's Bible Commentary and even the one volume set New Interpreters Commentary might be a little more user friendly but the whole 12 volume set may be over bearing. This matter of picking commentaries is very important because you don't want to misinterpret what the commentator is saying. There are people who are lost reading commentaries because they are missing pieces concerning the terms and expressions. For example if you see the term LXX which is not just letters it means Septuagint which is simple the Old Testament written in Greek we need to understand this while we are reading the commentaries so that we do not misunderstand the information. Here are some commentaries which is not an exclusive list but just a glimpse at different levels of works.

Beginners

Thru the Bible Commentary

Commentary Critical and Explanatory

Zondervan Bible Commentary

Believer's bible Commentary

Intermediate

The Pulpit Commentary

Holman's Bible Commentary

The Preacher's Commentary

The Expository Commentary

Advanced

New International Commentary of the New Testament

International Critical Commentary

Word Biblical Commentary

New Interpreter's Commentary

Languages

One of the advantages that I believe that some clergy possess is that they have spent their time being trained to fluently use the languages to capture the original meanings to the text of a particular manuscript. One thing that I will caution those who have not been seminary trained who attempt to use these languages is that a little Greek and Hebrew is dangerous in the hands of someone that doesn't know its power. It is my view that it is best not to use Greek and Hebrew oppose to using Greek and Hebrew and not use it with the accuracy that is needed in pronunciation and in interpretation. A preacher would do him or herself well to go and pick up Bill Mounce's book "Greek for the Rest of Us" if you want a couple of clues on how to deal with the languages. I warn you that for you to learn this art of using the languages correctly it takes discipline and drive on the behalf of the person.

While using the Biblical Language or the etymology in a passage limit yourself to about three to four Greek words that you use for the passage unless it is totally necessary to use more to arrive at a place of understanding for the pew. I read a Facebook posting that spoke about the uselessness of speaking Greek in the sermon. The writer articulated that the use of Greek and Hebrew in a sermon was to show off to the congregants what the person knew and not themselves. I believe that this statement is not true for everyone. I am of the persuasion that God desires for his church to be stretched and to continue to grow into the saving knowledge of Jesus Christ and if using Greek terms is how you accomplish that then it should be done to the best of the Preacher's ability.

Use the Greek to your advantage such as Christ's name. It is Christos (transliterated) meaning anointed one, which it has omicron sigma on the back which is in the second declension masculine and in the nominative case which is the subject of the sentence if it was grouped in a certain context. This knowledge can be used to really enlighten the assignment of Christ to people and the power of his position and the prophesies of old. Some believe Christ is Jesus last Name! Wow!! But it is his assignment.

One last component concerning Greek that I want to share is being careful not to Use the wrong sources. A preacher should not run to Strong's to get the meaning of Greek and Hebrew or illegitimate sources that give you the wrong interpretation that is dated such as some bible dictionaries that have inaccurate meanings.

Questions and Reflections

Do you believe the usage of Biblical language is important to exegesis? If so, why do you believe this?

Are you willing to discipline yourself to learn more about the languages?

What communities will you seek out to make sure your etymology pronunciations and usage of the language is correct?

Day Five Introduction and Putting the Pieces together

Chapter 8

I eluded to earlier that I look at the pieces that I have been collecting as a gigantic puzzle. Each day we have been collecting pieces this is why it is vitally important for the exegetical process that you document, document, document! When you have documented your quotes and your connecting scripture, your illustrations your points of application then it makes it easier to compile it and place it in it's proper place. When you get to Friday you can take your points and put them together as follows

Title: Specialized Support through the Sovereign

Proposition: Providence gives Provision through his Passionate Participation

Thesis: Provisions of God

Antithesis: Loses that we Take in Life (use this for the Introduction)

Raise Question: How does he support us beyond our offenses to the Sovereign?

I. **Supernatural Source**

II. **Saturated with Sin**

III. **Spotless Savior**

IV. **Sacredly Selected**

Above is the Outline that is used as the structure to hold everything together sense we have this we can now plug in the things from our research in order to put meat on the skeletal outline that we have. You must be creative in this process it is the job of the book to help you with this process not to give you every answer.

I heard a preacher say that there are no better sermons they are better libraries some of the lack of effective sermons is because we haven't made the upfront investment of purchasing books. My father Rev. Joseph Chapman speaks of this acquiring of books to his carpentry work he does around the house when I was younger. Rev. Chapman use to say as you study and work on your sermon, if you can't get to an answer that you are pursuing and you know that the answer is out there you need to add that book or tool to your tool box. The outline and its content is dependent upon the tools in the tool box. This is not to imply that God is not the main source of revelation that is not my point of view. I believe that when you have invested in excellent resources then you have more ideas that the creator will work with because you are honoring him through preparation.

This whole notion of preparation is not a one sided affair. God is expecting for you to invest in where he is taking you. He expects for you to be totally engaged in your mind, your heart, your emotion and your spirit. When you have the will power and the drive to perfect the process of preparation through sermon prep he will meet you before the moment and in the moment when you minister to his people. Be reminded he doesn't have to use anyone to get his will done he can be what my pastor articulates as an independent worker but he suffers it so for skin and sky to do spectacular things in society and the result is salvation of humanity.

Introduction

There are clergy who observe the introduction as the simplest part of the sermon process. In my experience that is dead wrong! The introduction is the most tedious part of the sermon. I view the introduction as what sets the tone to the entire sermon. You have three to five minutes to convince people that they ought to lend you their heart and their hearing for your heralding about heaven. If you don't intrigue them to listen on beyond this point then you can lose a soul for eternity. Wow this is serious business!

In speech Communication they have what is described as an attention getter! This attention getter is use to get the audiences attention. You can use several methods to get the audiences attention such as a: profound question, an abbreviated story that connects well with the topic, a possible illustration, and life experience. All of these will serve a preacher well if the story is told with eloquence and with the right pace and aim.

Another thing the introduction must have is a thesis or antithesis which will allow the preacher to connect one segment of attention getter to the thesis or antithesis. For this outlined aforementioned we will take the antithesis of the sermon for John 3:16. In this introduction we would speak about lost. We can begin with listing all of the things that have been lost: integrity, peace, love, patience, loyalty, economic status, marriages, ministries, identity etc.

We could continue with using phrases such as short end of the stick, being out numbered and outlasted, here is the **Transition:** out of all we have lost we have a God that while we are slipping he surely knows how to pick up the slack. This transition took me from the antithesis to the thesis because we can't forget that the title is we receive specialized support through the sovereign.

After we have made this transition we will insert the proposition next which was:

Proposition: <u>Providence</u> gives <u>Provision</u> through his <u>Passionate Participation</u>

Next is the raise Question which allows us to smoothly add our points by answering the question.

Raise Question: How does he support us beyond our offenses to the Sovereign?

After this then the Outline that has the meat on it will be inserted as follows:

I. **Supernatural Source**
II. **Saturated with Sin**
III. **Spotless Savior**
IV. **Sacredly Selected**

Please note when you give the points that you have don't be redundant and don't be dull when you give these particular points, you need to use verbiage like the first principle that John teaches us, the second principle John teaches us and so on but you want to make sure that you shift words around in order to have a smooth flow to what you desire to articulate.

The Sermon is Completed: Now that your sermon is completed it is time for you to step away from it for the rest of the day. I am thoroughly convinced that the manuscripts you have written are all eligible for revisions but they are not so clarion when you are closely involved in the work. It is liken unto Les Brown statement that you can pay attention to the story with detail when you are in the frame. You need to take time away from the document and have some fun doing other things; go and enjoy a hobby in order that you may take the time to refresh your prospective as well as clear your head for other possible thoughts that may come when you unclutter your mind.

There are times that we can push ourselves into a slump and so we need that time in which we allow for God to speak to us through nature, for God to speak to us through other people and possible a preacher that you can go and hear. You need to take the time and relax your mind so the next day you can concentrate on meditation and be ready to deliver.

Confirmation

There is a lost art form in preaching and that is to seek the confirmation of God over what you are preaching and teaching. I don't believe that it is totally up to us what we want to preach to God's people I believe there is a divine element involved in choosing the message to be delivered. There is definitely a designated people and a designated preacher that God has preordained in time that they need to meet and when they meet there is a certain kind of message that God has prepared the ground for. The message they will receive will be released just for them in order that they can do mighty exploit in His name. I don't believe in deja vu, I don't believe in luck, I don't believe in serendipitous spiritual response I don't support the notion of pick what worked at the last church.

I believe that you have to risk failure in order for God to favor your body of work or sermon. I remember hearing Abraham Smith say "sometimes to get better you have to risk failure do you hear me preachers." God knows exactly what he desires to be said and experienced and we need to give him total submission and give him the glorious goods. God is not concerned about your reputation as a preacher, God is not concerned about your name having notoriety, and God is not concerned in the creature comforts that you collect he wants the children of God to receive clear communication.

The question that is ringing in the souls of the ruptured that is attempting to find rest in the redeemer is, is there a word from the

Lord? The answer should be with no hesitation yes humanity still is receiving answers from heaven. Preach what the Lord has instructed you to preach and he will grant you victory upon victory upon victory I am surely a witness!

Questions and Reflections

How important is the introduction to the sermon?

What are the features to a strong introduction?

How will you keep your introductions fresh in the sermons to come?

If you do what is easy your life will be hard. If you do what is hard your life will be easy.

Les Brown

Meditation and the Delivery of the Message the Time is Here

Chapter 9

As a product of the African American Tradition of Preaching what is affectionately known as preaching in the black experience, auditory is just as important as the study itself. There are preachers that were well prepared through study but the delivery of their sermon were bland, which made the sermon fall flat on the ground because vocally the preacher didn't take us on the journey. So meditation is very important when we consider preaching in power.

During meditation we must be submissive to God. There must be an understanding that the one that is about to proclaim the message is just as much in need of the message as those in whom he or she is preaching it to. During meditation we remove the mask as I spoke about in the text "Preaching Without Heart". God at this time can remove and challenge us with no resistance concerning our mindset our behavior and even our motives for delivering the message he gave us. Larry Crabb says that the scholar is also the struggler when investigating these text.

When you are thinking of meditation that word biblically means to chew as a cow is chewing grass. As the cow chews the grass he swallows it then regurgitates it back up and chews on it some more and that is what we have to do. We as preachers we must find a sacred place of practice to chew on the pending delivered message. Some take a quiet drive and just speak their sermon out loud in the car; there are others that use washer machines as pulpits to speak the word just to hear it, and become more intone with the transitions shifts and rhythm of the sermon. What ever you do there is a zone you need to get into.

In the realm of professional sports the greats have a pregame workout. This is the regular routine for them prior to the battle on the court or field. Some of them listen to music to become amp, others will get to the stadium a 1hr and a half early to shoot or loosen up or even lift weights. The point is their trying to find a zone so that they can pour there all out on the activity they love.

Preachers we have more at stake then a trophy that is corruptible we have humanities souls and we need to be focused and discipline to get into a zone so that we can become in tune with God in order that we may preach with power and as I say each time I preach that God would take that which is prepared in private and display it on a public platform. You should meditate no less then three hours up to the time to preach because if your spirit is not right all your work will be for not.

If you are going to meditate you have to prepare your self for distractions. No one really wants to bother a preacher until its meditation time. All types of problems and challenges will arise before you have to deliver those are just contractions you have to stay focus on the delivery of the baby which is the sermon. Any one can be used as a distraction to get you off track so watch as well as pray.

In your meditation worship God; Enjoy the presence of God. Listen to music or ocean soundtracks something serene and think on the assignment that you have been given. Think on the privilege of just being chosen. Then speak life into your self you have to tell yourself that you are the vessel of God, that you are anointed for this hour to deliver a message. Blot out the voices that tell you that you are going to make mistakes or that you can't do this. NO ! NO! You have to take hold of your conscious mind and say I am who God says I am and I will make a difference!

I leave you with this Mike Tyson that Heavy Weight Juggernaut spoke about how he prepared for Fights. Tyson said every opponent he faced at the beginning he was terrified of these men but as he trained he became more confident. By the time it was fight night he says in the locker room he is still terrified but when it is time to walk to the ring he gets more confident with every step and when he gets into the ring has a metamorphosis into a boxing god and now I own this man.

When you prepare to preach you have to gain more confidence with each day of study; While you are driving to the church you may still lack confidence but when they come and get you to come to the sacred sanctuary with every step you ought to become more confident that you studied, you have something to say, you have something life changing to share, and when you get into the pulpit that God will empower you with his spirit to own the moment. Stop being afraid of the moment be afraid of the God who gave the moment.

We all get nervous but God gave you a chance and you ought to take advantage of it and give the best you got because You! Yes! You have something to offer I pray this book has helped you and I look to see what Greatness God is going to bring out of you to give to the world God bless!

Questions and Reflections

Do you know what meditation is? If so, how important is it to your preparation prior to the delivery of the sermon?

What new ways of meditation can you learn from if any?

When is the best time for you to meditate?

Greatness is when you consistently perform the things
you don't want to do but knowing you have to do them
joyfully and passionately. – Aaron Chapman

Defying the Ten Misnomers of Preaching

Chapter 10

We have charted our course together and made significant strides to better ourselves as preachers. There have been critical lessons that we have learned from this textual experience. In this final chapter, let us take a few moments to do a quick review of how far we have come. You should be proud of the progress that you have made toward being more proficient in your preaching presentation. We have learned:

Do not Despise the Process

Determining your Paradigm of Preaching

Developing Original thought in Sermon Preparation

Day One acqauiting yourself with the Text

Day Two Starting to Build the Bridge

Day Three the Meat of the Message Crafting Points

Day four Refine thoughts through Commentary and Etymology Study

Delivery and Meditating over the message, The Time is Here

Now that we have treaded back the thread of our experience; let us complete our dialogue surrounding preaching by discussing the topic of *defying the misnomers that come with the territory of preaching.* I am sure that there are preachers waiting for an opportunity to make a great impact in the vineyard which they have been planted. Although some preachers may initially have pure motives, they have been polluted by other prospectives of what ministry entails to make a profound impact as a preacher. Let us take a microscopic view of these misnomers!

1 My preaching can out live my daily living practice

It is shocking how preachers have purchased the satanic shares that they can preach with power and have a life exuding with spiritual bankruptcy. If you believe you can out preach your life your misinformed! When living an existence contrary to the will of God you will experience a cheap glory instead of the fullness of God's joy. Transparency before God will enable you to receive emotional, physological, and spiritual healing.

Countless Preachers have a tremendous gift that they use for the glory of God but they are found preaching without a contrite heart. God wants the man and not just the message; He wants the women not just the word; He desires the human and not just the heralding for heaven; he wants your soul and not just your sermon. A personal relationship that is pure and avaiable to God is what brings you to a place of power in your preaching.

Recently I heard a preacher exclaim that I would rather see a sermon lived any day than to hear a sermon preached. Congregants that converge weekly desire to know does the preacher have the goods! They yearn to know does the preacher have the passion that goes beyond public performance and his/her spiritual behavior is prevalently observed on the personal front porch of the preacher. Living a life style contrary to what you preach is giving the saints of God smoking mirriors and tricks. The preachers of the gospel must have a gospel that can break the yokes of bondage in their own lives as they are being empowered to effectuate change in others.

Our lives must bare the rhytemactic sound of righteousness, a rhetoric that captivates those who err on the side of their rascalities but they will become liberated because of our resounding truth which ushers in repentance. Walter Brueggeman states that he sees poets as prophets in his identification of Christ as the final poet. The poet / prophet is a voice that shatters settled reality and evokes now possibility in the listening assembly. Therefore let us live a lifestyle that is according to the word of God and let us watch the word work on our behalf.

#2 I must have a Biological Father or Mother Pastoring to be a Great Preacher

There is a blessing to have someone in ministry who is a trailblazer. Especially when the trailblazing is initiated by someone that has had a great involvement in bringing you into this world (Parents). Contrary to the thinking of some preachers there is a remnant of preachers that believe that they have a glass ceiling in ministry all because they don't have relatives that are pastors or national evangelist. Of course there are those who are related to those who are in places of power can use their influence to promote and push their family but it doesn't always turn out that way!

Let me tell you man or woman of God the Lord knew where he was going to place you before he placed you. The Lord predetermine the people he would allow to be in your circle of contact. The greatest source of reference for confidence for our minsitry is Jeremiah chapter one in that call narrative God knew him and us. This is the most Important! So often preachers focus on what they don't have (trailblazers in their family) oppose to the things that they do have going for them in ministry.

Often times we neglect the auspicious privelege to be the pace setter and the break through prodigy. There are times that the hills and the hurdles and the lack of opportunity builds a drive and persistence in you that can't be formed with every door of opportunity being opened for you. You can't dwell on what others have, the question is what do you have? What can you do? What are the choices that you can make? What are the sacrifices and the stance that you can take in order to become a catalyst for those whose normalcy is the personality of the least in ministry.

Preacher you may be called to travel the road least traveled. You may be the one that one writer states: don't follow the path but go to the place where there is no path and blaze a path there. There are times that God as John Mason wrote God does not desire for you to have a point of reference. In order for him to do the impossible he desires to use those who are ignorant to impossibility to make things possible.

3 I don't need to be educated in order to do effective ministry

According to Lincoln and Mamiya the postmodern African American clergy must be mentored and formally educated for the Black Church to advance (Lincoln and Mamiya 1990,399) They went further to express that if the level of academia doesn't become elevated they forecasted that the black church as we know it today can become none existent.

We live in a very different world compared to fourty to fifty years ago. There was a period in certain cultural ecclestiatical context that education didn't have much significants. This is not to suggest that there is no interest educationally. That would be a melicious lie! There were African American clergy who were indeed educated but it would be easier to find a unicorn then to find this demographic in the churches of old. Today there is a necessity for the clergy to carry a deep sense of the importance of education.

Congregants are no longer enthused exclusively with the emotional experience translated through whooping and hollaring and demonstrative expressions from the pulpit. They are saying that they want to be feed spiritually! This means give me relevatory information as my main course and the theatrics becomes the icing on the cake.

The question given rise is, is theological education for everyone, Absolutely Not! Although theological education is not for everyone there are theological concepts from the seminary that are transferable in any ministry context. Those who will lead the churches in the future must be solid doctrinally and theologically. The concentration of preachers should be to have value in their heads (intellect), hearts (passion), and the heavenly (spirit).

4 God knows my heart

This phraselogy "God knows my heart" has been used very often to excuse meaningless mediocrity in ministry. Indeed, the Lord knows our hearts but the Lord also knows our fruits. In ministry, we sometimes give ourselves a safety net and it is packaged in this verbage that the "Lord Knows my Heart".

You have to ask yourself if you have ever stretched yourself beyond comfort. Have you tried to accomplish something for God that was hard? Often we do not have an epiphany (moment) because we are operating in a quandrant that is safe and we label that corridor "God knows my heart!"

Take a moment and really think over the several opportunities that were left unfulfilled because you excused yourself! How many times did you give up short of the goal which was failure but you gave this filler God Knows my heart! We must have the conviction to not only allow the Lord to know our heart we ought to allow the world to see our heart through the discipline that we offer on a daily basis in the craft of ministry.

If you are honest we don't only tell ourselves this subconciously but we surround ourselves with people who use excuses to give us a way of escape. We must not accept the claim ticket to remove us from accepting the responsibility to fulfill the capacity that is enveloped inside of us. The next time we are given this phrase "God knows my heart" use it as fuel to check your determination, to remove your limits from your mind, and to become the launching pad to have a more caliberated push toward your potential. Be true to your heart but don't allow your emotions to manipulate your progress on the journey.

#5 I have to have a little dirt on Me to fit in

There are so many people whose sin to their destiny is conformity. They forfeit the identity and become attracted and allurded to the false self. Henri Nouwen calls this compulsion desiring more of the same things that perpetuate the heartbreaks and the brokenness that has left preachers limp and paralyzed in their progress.

Unfortunately I believe that riotous living is an imperceptible issue that is masked in the church but people are recruited to engage in conformity. There is spiritual bullying that I believe exist in the church. Just as children are picked on or intentionally bothered. Everyday these students have to maintain under unnecessary irritates for being who they are, this is also true among Preachers. There are preachers that will defame; belittle and verbally abuse you if you don't engage in the practices that they believe are priority.

Many preachers have fallen into this fog of trying to fit in because they desire to fulfill their feeling of belonging. It is tremendously difficult for those pecuilar preachers to pivot their way toward another path because they believe their futures are predicated on those in the *in* crowd. I want you to know that you need to have the courage and stand up and be what God has called you to be. If you take a pregnant moment to ponder you are the most effective and happy when you were being who you are instead of what they desire you to be.

There is no prerequiste that you have to engage in any cursing; fornicative; in appropriate exploits in order for you to become the preacher that God has called for you to be. In order for you to obtain what others don't have you have to do what others will not do according to Les brown. Sometimes we are running in the pack when God is looking for us to actually lead in the pack.

I believe there is someone that is trying to fit in and size up when God wants you to know he has created you wonderfully and carefully. Your validation comes from your Creator and he will make it his business to have your vision of your life come to pass!

6 Preachers do not have to be nice

I have heard it expressed from the pulpit that preachers don't have to be nice. I believe if we are going to use this verbage we then have to delineate what does nice mean. The definition for nice is pleasant, kind, and delightful. Who wants to listen to a preacher who doesn't desire to be nice. If we want to stretch this a little further I believe that these are the characteristics of Jesus Christ.

There must be a proclivity to be who we are and not try to act a certain way because others that are gifted that we possible admire act in obnoxious ways. If you love laughter then laugh that is who you are; if you are very emotional then you need not suppress that emotion because it is not in the holy grail of preacherdom (What ever that is). I believe that the Lord is amused at our behavior that we believe will make us into someone great instead of being who we are at the depth of our personality

I want to challenge every preacher reading this text to go out of your way to be kind to people. We ought to be servant leaders awaiting the opportunity to serve others to make their lives more spiritually fulfilled. We have never lived if we have not yet served someone else. There is a kind word you can share, there is a listening ear that you can offer, and there is wisdom that we can impart to others if we just be who we are in God.

Whenever you approach another preacher and you call him or her too nice think on these words. Don't criticize the preacher for being longsuffering or sincere because both of these traits are a runway to being blessed beyond imagination in the eyes of God. Find someone today that you can show his lovingkindness.

7 I Have to be a Road Evangelist to be Successful

There appears to be so much confusion that circles around the calling that God Has place in a preachers life. This confusion is not merely by accident this can stimulate from people who program you to believe there is only one way to truly be successful. The tough part to this realization is that preachers and mentors will impress upon you that there is more than one rounte for ministry but they elude to the foremore as the ultimate gift. Knowingly or even unknowly we are put in a box that success can only be derive from one place.

In my denomination and culture the National Evangelist is suppose to be the cream dala crumb of the preachers. There is a mindset that you have not made it in ministry or excelled to the apecs of ministry until you have flown around the country and have a jammed schedule packed with churches that hear you speak yearly.

On one occasion I had the opportunity to speak with a younger preacher and we begin to speak about the signs of a successful ministry. I begin informing him that success can come in various forms such as seminary professor, pastoring, evangelist, president of a university, author etc. I could hear a pin drop on the phone this was how silent he was. I attempted to advise him concerning the importance of identifying your gifting and going after it wholeheartedly.

TD Jakes says do not let anyone define you because when they define you they incarcerate you and then put a period when there should be a comma. I believe this is a profound statement because I believe that when you have your identity in Christ and you are flowing in your gifting you can flow in more then one area. No one can determine if you are cut out for something except God because based on your fruits it will show. People always desire to tell you what you can not do because they become one demensional but I have discovered you can be a seminary professor, evangelist and an author and much more because you found there was more than one way to success.

Learn how to find your gifting and identity in him and you are guarenteed to make an impact in someones life because you have found what makes you a success in God's eyes and that is stirring up every gift He deposited in you!

8 God honors me ditching my family while delivering others

There is an emphasis in scripture concerning priortitizing the preachers home life. 1 Timothy 3:5 NRSV says if a man (woman) cannot manage his own household, how can he/she take care of God's church? I believe that it is clear that God's desire is for us to maintain healthy relationships in our domestic setting.

Ministers for whatever reason believe that they have to have either or in ministry. They can have the church or they can have their family. This way of thinking is skewd because God wants us to model healthy decisions spiritually. One of the ways that we can model this behavior is through our daily action in our personal lives.

Let me ask you are you selling out your relationship with your family for ambition and opportunity? Do you carry a healthy balance? I am totally sensitive to the call of God that is on the lives of those that minister in a impactful way. We can not use preaching as a idol god which we neglect the commitment and the promise that we have made to our family.

So many individuals who are connected with a preacher that does not make his family a priority. Children have went without their parent; wives and husbands have had to settle for only a form of marriage oppose to what they really thought that they were going to experience. Preachers must make a decision that we can't have our cake and eat it to. I heard Les brown quote another speaker who said life is short eat the desert first. We can enjoy the life that God has for us with and without the church and be an example of someone that is tremendously spiritual but have their feet on the ground at the same time.

9 Sermon Pirating is acceptable - everyone has done it

Sermon Pirating is something that many people want to avoid speaking about. I am very comfrotable in speaking about plagarizing sermons because I believe that it is my fudiciary responsibility to be the eyes and ears of heaven to steer clergy in the right direction. I have the plum pleasure to engage in pedagogical practice to upcoming preachers in seminary and in the ecclestiastical context. It is my calling to coach and mentor preachers so they can be the best they can be in God.

Unfortunately we have many people that have turned a blind eye to these issues. Dr. Martin Luther King stated injustice anywhere is injustice everywhere. I believe that the same principles ring true when it comes to the confiscating of sermons that were not written by the individual. Pastor Gardner Calvin Taylor the former Pastor of the Concord Church in New York city stated that when someone steals a sermon it is like them taking a child away from the crib of the preachers sermonic thought.

I feel compelled to let you know preacher to preacher that I know that the task that we are up against is no easy task. Dr. Ralph West says that every time the preacher has preached a part of him or her dies. We have a great price to pay as a preacher but the reward of seeing transformed lives make all the difference.

It may be safe to say that if you feel as if you have to pirate sermons in order for you to keep up then you have too many task before you. Here are some clues of how you can avoid sermon pirating. First, come up with a disciplined schedule in which you do what Erik Thomas calls -- learn how to pass. Everything that people want to involve you in - learn how to pass. Secondly, you have to learn how to delegate responsibilities. This enables you to train yourself out of a job. Thirdly, you have to believe that everything that the Lord has put in you is good enough for the people to receive it. This is not an extensive list of things to do but I pray that this will assist in your effort to be true before God in your preparation moments.

10 Earning Degrees automatically makes me into a great preacher

Degrees don't equate anointing or effectiveness in pulpit performance. I would in a heart beat tell a preacher don't go to school if you believe that the degrees will help you become a great preacher. Theological school can sharpen the focus and the skills that you have presently but it is not the sine qua non of great preaching.

Theological school teaches you how to be discipline and think theologically such as Howard and Duke speak about in that fantastic read "How to think theologically". There must be a work ethic that must merge with the educational prowess that will give you a good mixture to become a preacher that excells. Becoming a great preacher happens when you can engage in the behavior pattern previously mentioned and search out those who are already performing at that level and begin to glean the knowledge that they have. Preachers so often marvel at greatness but never learn the steps of how do they transform themselves into the preacher they know is on the inside.

Let's face it many only want to work for a temporal time but desire timeless results that is not how the ministry works. The reality is the more that you are willing to give up and invest in your ministry is the greater chance that you will have to achieve the set goals that you have in ministry. So often preacher's go to school and get to commencement and they become parked. The objective of some preachers are to go to school just to have a piece of paper and not fulfilling the potential that is untapped deposited by providence. What a mistake!

What a waste of money to go to school for a piece of paper alone; that money could have been used for something else. It is the journey of the man and woman that transforms you into who you are not the degree that makes this accomplishment significant.

Do not get me wrong, I am pro-school everyday of the week but make sure that when you go it is a God move and not a prestige move! It takes passion to go through degree programs trust me I know I have three humble under my belt and attempting to ignore the itch to get another one! I believe there has to be purpose behind our pondering and not proceeding prematurely which is not a move soaked in productivity but in futile activity. Education should be used to tap into your potential to illuminate your purpose that has been etched in your heart by the hands of God!

Questions and Reflections

Have you accepted any of the misnomers mentioned?

How would you describe success in preaching ministry?

Who will you influence in order to begin to remove these toxic misnomers?

Biography

Dr. Aaron L. Chapman, a servant of God, is often referred to as a relevant power packed Minister of the priceless Gospel of our Lord and Savior Jesus Christ.

An alumnus of Murray Wright High School, Rev. Chapman graduated in the top five percent (5%) of his class. He was accepted to Eastern Michigan University, and shortly thereafter his academic achievement was further honored by being placed on the Dean's list. In December 2003, he received a Bachelor of Science Degree in Communications with a Minor in General Business from Eastern. In January 2004, he began his pursuit for a Dual Master's Degree in Divinity and Theology at Ashland Theological Seminary. In June 2006, Rev. Chapman graduated with honors from Ashland with a Masters of Divinity Degree. In his desire to be all that God had called him to be, Dr. Aaron L. Chapman in 2011 received an earned Doctoral Degree from Ashland Theological Seminary.

At present, Dr. Chapman serves as a professor in Homiletics at Ashland Seminary and a professor at the Heritage Center in Denominational Studies and several other educational institutions including: Ecumenical Seminary, Grace College, Manthano College, Triumph Church Institute, Michigan North Central Ecclesiastical

Jurisdiction (Bishop Sheard presiding) and his very own Seminary on Wheels. He is also the Author of the newly released books "Preaching without Heart" and "I'm Called to Preach: Now What?"

Dr. Aaron L. Chapman served as a faithful member of Galilee Missionary Baptist Church for eleven (11) years where he was called to preach the gospel under the tutelage of Rev. Dr. Tellis J. Chapman. On April 23, 2005. God called him to Pastor the Dedicated To Christ Baptist Church. Dedicated To Christ held their first worship service on September 4, 2005, at 19400 Evergreen in Detroit, Michigan in the St. Timothy Lutheran Church. Through the grace of the Lord and Leadership of Dr. Aaron L. Chapman, Dedicated To Christ purchased their new church home at 4424 8th Street in Ecorse Michigan in October, 2007.

Within the ranks of the local, State, and National Conventions and Congresses, Dr. Chapman is the Congress President for the Central District Association, Homiletics Instructor for BM&E State Convention, and has received Christian Education certificates in the Holy Spirit Doctrine; Building Effective Ministries and Pastors Seminars.

Since the inception of Dedicated to Christ, Dr. Chapman has established several ministries: Drama Ministry, Evangelism, Media, Music/Praise Ministry, Nurses, Operation Bread Basket, Operation "Big Give", Recreation, Security, Shepherds Care, Dedicated To Christ Bookstore, DTC Café, Men, Women and Youth Ministries, Dance Ministry, Stick Squad, Audio/Visual Ministry, Godly Guidance Ushers Ministry, IPH After school program, My Bridges (DHS), Dedicated to Christ Website, Dedicated to Christ phone app and Destine For Greatness Childcare. For five (5) years he has served as founder and leader of Dedicated to Christ's Biblical Impartation Class.

Dr. Aaron Chapman is married to the former Valarie Kay Wilkinson and they are the proud parents of two children Aaron Christian and Destiny Kay Chapman.

Reference

Crabb, Larry 1999. *The Safest Place on Earth*. Nashville: Word Publishing.

Detz, Joan. 2014. *How to write & Give a Speech*. New York: St. Martin's Griffin.

Droge, A.J. 1992. "Apologetics." *Anchor Bible Dictionary*, Vol. 4, 302. New York, NY: Doubleday Publisher.

Duke, James O. and Stone 2006. *How to Think Theologically*. Minneapolis: Fortress Press.

Foster, Richard 1988. *Celebration of Discipline*. New York: Harper San Francisco.

Fred, Craddock 2010. *Preaching*. Nashville: Abingdon Press.

Gardner, Taylor 1977. *How Shall They Preach*. Elgin,IL: Progressive Baptist Publishing House.

Gibbs, A.P. 2002. *The Preacher and his Preaching*. Kansas City: Walter Publishers

Gorman, Michael J. 2009. *Elements of Biblical Exegesis*. Peabody, Massachusetts: Hendrickson Publishers.

Johnson, Graham 2001. *Preaching to a Postmodern World*. Grand Rapids: Baker Books.

King, Martin L. 1963. *Strength to Love*. Philadelphia: Fortress Press.

Koller, Charles W. 1964. *How to Preach Without Notes*. Grand Rapids. Baker Academic.

Lincoln, Eric and Lawrence Mamiya.1990. *The Black Church in the African American experience*. Durhamad, London: Duke University Press.

Lunsford, Andrea 2001. *The Everyday Writer*. New York: Bedford/ ST. Martin's.

Mason, John 1996. *Conquering an Enemy called Average*. Tulsa Oklahoma: Insight International.

Maxwell John C. 1999. *Think on these Things*. Kansas City: Beacon Hill Press.

McMickle, Marvin 2001. *Living Water for Thirsty Souls*. Valley Forge, PA: Judson Press.

McClure, John 2007. *Preaching Words*. Louisville London: Westminster John Knox Press.

Massey, James 1980. *Designing the Sermon*. Nashville: Abingdon Press.

Osborne, Grant R. 1991 *The Hermeneutical Spiral*. Illinois : InterVarsity Press.

Proctor Samuel D. 1994. *The Certain Sound of the Trumpet*. Valley Forge, PA: Judson Press.

Robinson, Haddon. 2001. *Biblical Preaching*. Grand Rapids. Baker Academic.

Rummage Stephen N. 2002. *Planning Your Preaching*. Grand Rapids: Kregel Publications.

Wilson, Paul S. 1995. *The Practice of Preaching*. Nashville TN.: Abingdon Press.